THE WINDOW OF THE
LORD'S
RETURN

2012 – 2020

ARE WE THE
TRIBULATION GENERATION?

—JOHN SHOREY—

HigherLife Development Services
Oviedo, Florida

Window of the Lord's Return, 2012 - 2020
By John Shorey

Published by HigherLife Development Services, Inc.
400 Fontana Circle
Building 1 --- Suite 105
Oviedo, FL 32765
(407) 563-4803
www.ahigherlife.com

ISBN-13: 978-1-939183-07-1
ISBN 10: 1-939183-07-3

Cover Design: David Whitlock
Printed in the United States of America
Copyright© August 2010

Second printing June 2011
Third printing   March 2012
Fourth printing May 2012
Fifth printing   June 2012
Sixth printing   July 2012
Seventh printing November 2012

TABLE OF CONTENTS

Letters From the Pulpits to the Pews. 1

Introduction. 7

1. Could We be Wrong About A Pre-Tribulation Rapture?. 11

2. A Needed Second Look at the Rapture 21

3. The Sealing of the 144,000 and Other Pre-Rapture Events . . .33

4. How Does the United States Fit into the Prophetic Picture? . .43

5. God's "No Man Left Behind". 49

6. Can Gentiles be Saved After the Rapture? 55

7. Other Bible Teachers' Perspectives Concerning the Rapture . . .59

8. The Coming Antichrist. 79

9. Pre-vs.-Mid-Tribulation View of the Rapture 89

10. Mid-Tribulation Rapture? I Make my Case 121

11. Post-Tribulation View of the Rapture. 141

12. A Warning to Those Who Add or Subtract from God's Word . . 149

13. Can We Know When the Lord is Actually Coming? 157

14. The Window of the Lord's Return 165

15. Possible Scenario Story Leading to the Rapture 183

16. How to Prepare for the Last Days. 207

17. Closing Thoughts About the Lord's Return 221

ACKNOWLEDGMENTS

I would like to thank a few of those who have continued with me as I have worked on this study. Those who gave me their opinions and encouragement were:

My wife Shawnette, Betty Bransford, Ron LaVoie, Robert Casey, Lottie Holland, Ivan Secord, Jerry Logue, Greg Foster and Chuck Lorentzen,

A special thanks to Ron LaVoie, my computer technician.

LETTERS FROM THE
PULPITS TO THE PEWS

I have known John Shorey since 1974 and have always observed his very careful and considerate study of the Word of God. Therefore, I feel sure that this venture into the subject of the prophetic future is accompanied by much prayer and careful study of God's Word. It is a task most men would try to avoid, for the task is awesome, and the message often is rejected by the rank and file of Christianity.

Based upon the serious situations simmering in our world, his writings make the reader determine to be all God would have him to be as the time-clock moves closer to midnight.

May we determine to have oil in our lamps, trimmed and shining brightly, until that day.

Reverend Jack and Betty Bransford
Retired pastors and former Alaska District Superintendent of the Assembly of God

---

Dear Brother John,

I am an Assembly of God pastor, I grew up in the Assemblies from a child, and we have always believed and were taught that the church would not have to go through the seven year tribulation period. We would be caught up in the air with Christ and escape this period. After reading your book and searching the scriptures, I am convinced that we will not be pre-raptured before this period of time. It looks like the scriptures are saying the Rapture will occur somewhere around the sealing on the 144,000 Jewish missionaries. Wow, what an eye-opener. Thank you so much for all your hard work. Now mine is just beginning!

Thanks for laboring and putting the scriptures together where even a man, who from childhood was taught differently, can make sense of it all.

I will be ordering five books to start because I must get some key people on my side here in the church. You know what I mean I'm sure.

In Jesus Christ's Service,
~Pastor Bill

John,

As I told you at the onset of our recent phone conversation, I had come to a place several years ago, to see more of a "mid-trib" rapture as a result of a series of sermons I preached on the book of Revelation.

Your book brought all of that back to me, but with many more of the "blanks" filled in. How significant is the instruction God gave to Daniel clearly telling him that certain details of the end were to be "sealed up" until the end was near, which is obviously the time we are presently living in. I know how difficult it will be for mainstream Pentecostals to even "open" their hearts and minds to the possibility of a change in their theology concerning the Rapture. I know, our movement (A/G) has prided themselves on being doctrinally pure in this area, having never altered their pre-trib position in almost 100 years, or since the inception of the Assemblies of God fellowship. They guard and protect all our doctrines – 16 Fundamental Truths—with a vengeance. I am praying, along with you, that the Holy Spirit will get through to some of our key leaders, and your book will "fall" into their hands and into their hearts. How significant it is that Jim Bakker has received your message. He certainly does have an international reach. I have always felt a mandate from God to preach Christ's coming to the church and urge them to be "ready" and "prepared" to meet the Lord VERY SOON. I will continue to do that with even more urgency and conviction.

Blessings!
~Pastor Cal

Hi Brother John Shorey,

I received your book last Saturday. I have a "Bible Institute" degree from Liberty University, and I have studied prophecy since 1994.

Thanks be to God that he used you to write this book! I believe the Holy Spirit has used you to write this book and do surgery in detail to the Book of Revelation and events soon to occur. I have already read to page 128, and it is hard to put it down!

You make a compelling case for the mid-tribulation rapture as I have not ever read before! And you prove it by using and allowing the Bible to interpret it by the Old Testament, giving meaning to the New Testament and vice-versa which I believe is the right method of interpretation. The Window of the Lord's Return is a masterpiece for the End Times.

Glory to God!
~Antonio

John,

I obtained this book about a month ago. I started reading it one night and literally couldn't put it down until I had finished it. I have always had so many questions about the timing of the rapture--even after attending Bible School, hearing many sermons and teachings, and studying the Word myself over the years. I believe the Lord has really blessed John with fresh understanding on this subject. After being so inspired, I called him and ordered 40 copies and have been handing them out to my pastor friends and to anyone who has an open mind. I really have had some positive feedback. This to me is a real must read. Thanks, John, for being obedient and taking the time and effort to write this book.

~Jerry

If you are a born again Christian, you have often heard about the Rapture and you probably believe it will happen before the Great Tribulation. That has been my belief for over 35 years, but not anymore. John Shorey in his thorough study of end time events has helped me to see the truth that we will not be living in heaven during the first half of this earth-shaking seven year period. I recommend you read this book, check every Bible verse, make spiritual and physical preparations, and share it with your family, pastor and friends.

We need not be surprised as these near future events begin to happen. If we heed Jesus' words to watch, be not deceived, beware, be ready and hear what the Spirit says to the churches. I pray that you will give John Shorey the opportunity to help you take a second look at the timing of the Rapture, have a more accurate understanding of the scriptures, and seriously consider the warning signs of our times.

~Charles

This is one of the most riveting books I have ever read. I read all the scriptures in the Bible, and they back up everything John Shorey says. For the many of us who have been taught and believed in the pre-trib theology, this book will open our hearts and minds to a different belief. God bless John Shorey for writing this book in obedience to God's urging.

~Bonnie

Since watching John Shorey on the Jim Bakker show I had to have this book. It has changed my view of the last days. I am happy that John has opened my eyes to what the Bible really says about the End Times.

~Joseph

Hi John,

Your book has opened up a new avenue for study. I have enjoyed reading your book and studying with a whole new outlook on the timing of the end time events.

The thing I like most about your book is that it does not tell us how to believe, or that we should believe in Mid-Tribulation. It gives us "Food for Thought" that we can study for ourselves. It leaves me wondering where we went wrong in our study to start with. Why, with all the well-educated and highly respected ministers that are preaching today, have we not heard more preaching about this?

I have to say, John, You have done a very good job putting this book together. I can tell that you have spent a lot of time in prayer and did a great deal of time studying to do this. I thank God for godly men like you who are willing to share your thoughts and put them into a book for all to read. That gives us a chance to study and make our own minds up as to what we believe for ourselves.

I pray that your book will reach many readers all over the world and give them "Food for Thought." You have made a believer of me!

Thank you and may God richly bless you and your family,
~Lois

John

I saw you on Jim Bakker's show and downloaded your book on my Kindle. I just finished reading it and am speechless. You are right - we have not been taught truth. You make it so plain; we definitely are going to go through part of the Tribulation. I have always had questions when I was told the opposite but didn't know the Word well enough to argue it. Thank you for writing this book. I pray every person on earth reads it.

Thank you.
~Donna

INTRODUCTION

For centuries Christians have asked the question, "When will the Lord return?" I have written this book, *The Window of the Lord's Return*, because I believe I can present evidence from scripture and from the signs of the times that the Lord could return during this coming window of time between 2012 - 2020. Please allow me to introduce my thoughts here.

It is my conviction that when Israel became a nation in 1948, a time-clock was started, and this generation will not pass away until the return of the Lord Jesus. Recently, I heard Reverend John Hagee say that we are the "Terminal Generation." I believe he meant that this generation will live to see the coming of the Lord. Since 1948, sixty-four years of this generation have expired. In chapter Thirteen of this book, I will present a strong argument for my position that seventy years is the length of a generation.

Some will ask, "Where do you see the Bible teach that Israel would be restored as a nation in the last days?" First, we need to look at Ezekiel 36:24 (KJV), *"For I will take you from among the heathen, and gather you out of all countries, and will bring you into your own land."*

Then look at Matthew 24:32-34. *Learn this lesson from the fig tree: As soon as its twigs get tender and its leaves come out, you know that summer is near. Even so, when you see all these things, you know that it is near, right at the door.* ***I tell you the truth; this generation will certainly not pass away until all these things have happened.***

The reference to the fig tree is referring to the nation of Israel, and figs refer to the people of Israel. I will show Bible references to support this teaching. The following verses in Joel 1:6-7 (KJV) show that Israel, the land that belongs to God, will be laid waste. This land is described as the fig tree, a fig tree that died. *For a nation is come upon my land, strong and without number, whose teeth are the teeth of a lion, and he hath the cheek teeth of a great lion. He hath laid my vine waste and barked my fig tree: he hath made it clean bare, and cast it away: the branches thereof are made white.*

The next verse I will use will show that the people of Israel were referred to as figs. They would be judged and removed from their land and dispersed around the world in judgment from God. Jeremiah 24:8-9 (KJV), *"And as the evil figs, which cannot be eaten, they are so evil; surely thus saith the LORD, So will I give Zedekiah the king of Judah, and his princes, and the residue of Jerusalem, that remain in this land, and them that dwell in the land of Egypt: And I will deliver them to be removed into all the kingdoms of the earth for their hurt, to be a reproach and a proverb, a taunt and a curse, in all the places whither I shall drive them."*

In 1948, the Children of Israel were allowed to return to the land of Israel. Note in Matthew 24:32: ***When you see the branches get tender and its leaves come out ...,*** **this is referring to life coming back to the fig tree or Israel, which was fulfilled in 1948.** When you look at Joel 1:6-7 (above), you see that when the nation of Israel was brought back to life, it was referred to as the fig tree. This "land" is also referred to as the land that belongs to God, also called Israel.

In this study, I will be looking at this narrowing window of time and attempt to show how close we could be to the Lord's return. I will also be sharing an in-depth study on the Rapture and other related end-time subjects. One of the subjects that I will be covering is the timing of the Rapture in relation to the Great Tribulation. I realize that this is a sensitive subject for many. Please realize that the timing of the Rapture has no bearing on our salvation, but it is important that we get it right.

I was reared mostly in the Catholic church (my mother's choice) where I never heard anything about end time doctrines. My father came from a large Protestant Christian family. It was from his family that I was first exposed to end-times doctrines. When I became a Christian in 1974, the church was all abuzz about the Rapture and imminent return of Jesus Christ. So, early in my new Christian walk, the Rapture doctrine and the book of Revelation caught my attention and have been an area of interest throughout my Christian life. I have heard some great preaching on the subject, mostly years ago. It is interesting, now that we are so close to the return of Christ, that we do not seem to hear as much preaching on the subject. Why is that? Could it be that many prophets of our time have been wrong, and sayings like, "You are as slow as the Second Coming," have made some steer away from this important end-time teaching? Could it be that some think that end-time events are too negative a subject and that the church is so caught up in the things of the world and keeping up with the Joneses that we do not want to hear this message that would disrupt our lives? I was recently told by an evangelist friend of mine that he was told by some churches that preaching on the End Times is off limits. They want feel-good messages and messages on prosperity.

I have studied this subject intently over the years, and have come up with some interesting thoughts. This book is presented to you as a journey. You will find some questions presented in the first few chapters are answered later in the book. When I combine my study in the Word of God with current events as they are, I am seeing so many of the parts of the mystery of the Lord's return coming together. I feel God's direction to share them with others; I believe God is trying to tell us something. I am convinced that we do not want to get caught unprepared for these coming events.

I have separated these thoughts into a few individual, separate discussions, and you can decide if they all fit together.

During the four years that I have worked on this book, I sent segments of the writing to friends whom I highly respect to seek out their opinions and insights. Some comments have been shallow, but the majority of the responses I received have been very positive.

The question that each of us needs to ask ourselves is this—do we really *want* to know the truth about the biblical timetable for the Rapture and the End Times? Allow me to illustrate.

Years ago, while attending the University of Alaska in Fairbanks, I had a few incredible opportunities to witness to many "high-up" Mormon leaders. I will not go into the names of the individuals, but one invitation was from an astronaut who landed on the moon. On another occasion, I was meeting with the ward president and former ward president of the Ketchikan, Alaska Mormon Church. I attempted to show them proof that the Book of Mormon originated from a plagiarized work of a minister who wrote the story from which the Book of Mormon was created before it came into the hands of Joseph Smith. I had the proof of government handwriting experts, and I was ready to show these two men, but they refused to look at the evidence because they did not want to see something different from what they had been taught.

I believe it is our tendency to have a similar attitude. It can be difficult to look intently into a teaching on a subject that you've adopted as truth and believed in for years. Let us consider that the Bible admonishes us in 2 Timothy 2:15 (KJV) to *Study to show thyself approved unto God, a workman that needeth not to be ashamed, rightly dividing the word of truth.* It is interesting what is said in Daniel, *"...the truth of this prophecy would be sealed until the time of the end...* So since we have been trying to explain the return of Christ for hundreds of years, could it be possible that we have made some mistakes? Is studying and rightly dividing the word of truth concerning the biblical prophecies of the End Times important enough to take a serious second look at from time to time? I believe it is.

CHAPTER ONE

COULD WE BE WRONG ABOUT A PRE-TRIBULATION RAPTURE?

C ould it be possible that many mainstream churches have taken an incorrect doctrinal position on the End Times for their churches? Is there a chance that a doctrine on the Rapture and the imminent return of Christ is based on incomplete information and poor interpretation of scripture?

I do not understand why it is so hard for us to accept the fact that we do not always get our theology right. Throughout church history, time has had a way of revealing the truth and correcting our errors. Based on what Jesus said about John, Jesus' disciples thought that Jesus would return in their lifetime. All but one of Jesus' disciples were martyred, and they were wrong about the timing of Christ's return.

Then replacement theology came along, which teaches that the nation of Israel was rejected by God and was replaced by the church; therefore, Israel did not have to be reborn as a nation. Again, they were wrong.

Then almost two hundred years ago, John Darby had a revelation that said that Christ would return for His bride before the seven year Great Tribulation started. His teaching, along with the dream of a teenage girl, switched the church from a mid-tribulation view of the Rapture to a pre-tribulation view. If you research and study the history of the pre-tribulation view of the Rapture, you will see it was cloaked in confusion and disagreement. Over time, this change in doctrine was accepted because it sounded good and made people feel comfortable. Just because a doctrine sounds good does not make it right.

What I have discovered in sharing the first printing of this book with pastors is that pastors are not generally open to the possibility that they have taught a doctrine on Christ's coming that could be flawed. Sid Roth wrote a book called *They Thought for Themselves*. This book is about Jews who have discovered Jesus as their Lord because they thought for themselves. It is interesting the reaction I get from lay Christians who are students of the Word and have an open mind to read this study. I hear comments like the following all the time: "I read it twice, I looked up the Bible verses, I believe you are right, and I just cannot believe we didn't see it." A friend with whom I attended college told me, "John, when I saw where you were going with the mid-tribulation view of the Rapture, I did not want you to be right, but after I studied your position, I have to say, I believe you are right." **One Christian leader told me. "If anyone will read your book with an open mind, they will get it. The case for the mid-tribulation Rapture is so plain in your book."**

When I went to Northwest Bible College, one of the top doctrinal professors told us that the rapture doctrine is most popular in America. In many parts of the world, Christians have suffered and are suffering persecution, hunger, and martyrdom on a daily basis. It is interesting that American Christians believe so strongly that God would never allow His people to suffer and go through tribulation. We have lost sight of the fact that in the early church, many of Christ's disciples were martyred. We should all read the book *Foxe's Book of Martyrs*. We would realize that when the church was standing up to persecution, the fruit of their lives was the salvation of souls.

Could the church be wrong about the timing of the Rapture? If so, what would be the ramifications of this mistake? Please do not be offended if my conclusions fly totally contrary to what most Christian churches believe. I have been exploring this question from the beginning of this study, and I am seeing too many scriptures that do not add up, building a strong case that we will not see a pre-tribulation Rapture.

In all sincerity, I really would like someone to show me why I am wrong in my interpretation because I would much rather see a pre-tribulation rapture as opposed to going through part of the Great Tribulation. One question has to be asked: "Is it possible to misread God's Word and have a belief system based on the poor interpretation of God's Word?"

Here is an example from John 14:2-3 (KJV): *In my Father's house are many mansions; if it were not so, I would have told you. I go to prepare a place for you and if I go and prepare a place for you, I will come again and receive you to myself, that where I am, there you may be also.*

Many Christians read this and believe that we will all have a mansion in heaven. In fact, hymns and songs have been written enforcing this belief. If you read this verse carefully, you will see that this verse does not say that we will all have a mansion. What it says is, *"In my Father's house are MANY mansions..."* Many mansions does not mean that all places in heaven are mansions. In Hollywood, there are many mansions, but all homes in that area are not mansions. The Word goes on to say, *"I go to prepare a place for you . . ."* The key word here is "PLACE." A place could be a tent and a cot. Does not God's Word teach us that we can lay up treasures in heaven? It is similar to having a heavenly bank account. Does not the Word say that only what is done for Christ will last? If your place in heaven is based on your heavenly bank account, do you believe you will have a mansion or a tent waiting for you?

If you are still not convinced that we will not all have a mansion in heaven you should read 1 Corinthians 3:12-15: *For no one can lay any foundation other than the one already laid, which is Jesus Christ. If any man builds on this foundation using gold, silver, costly stones, wood, hay, or straw, his work will be shown for what it is, because the Day will bring it to light. It will be revealed with fire, and the fire will test the quality of each man's work. If what he has built survives, he will receive his reward.*

If it is burned up, he will suffer loss, he himself will be saved, but only as one escaping through the flames.

I have received some comments, saying that I should not burst people's bubbles, but I should only teach words of comfort. I am sorry, but I disagree. I feel too many preachers have watered down their preaching instead of being honest with their flocks. When we arrive in eternity, would you want to be found guilty of holding back the truth? People need to realize that only what is done for Christ will count. Life is short, and we need to be sure we are burning our candle for God

I believe the most important book we should ever read is the Bible, inspired and breathed into his chosen writers to deliver the Word of God to man. I believe a mistake we can make is to take the writings and teachings of man as gospel-truth, instead of checking these teachings against the Word of God. In the New Testament, during the time of Paul, when he was preaching to the Bereans, Paul gave us a good example to follow. Acts 17:11: *Now the Bereans were of more noble character than the Thessalonians, for they received the message with great eagerness and examined the Scriptures every day to see if what Paul said was true.*

A book I recently read is a good example of why we need to examine what we read against what God's Word says. This book was about the Rapture and the End Times, written by a well-known teacher and preacher, a man I highly respect. In his chapter on the Rapture of the church, he says that 2 Thessalonians assures its readers that no saint will experience the seven-year Great Tribulation. The author does not quote chapter and verse to back up this statement. After reading 2 Thessalonians, I could not find any verse to back up this statement. We need to be like the Bereans, who search the scriptures to see if the Word of God backs up what our Bible teachers are telling us. Please do not question my motives for using real examples. The author of that book is a great teacher, but I am finding that even great teachers can be wrong in their interpretations of the Bible. I am sure that I will have mistakes pointed out to me as well.

As I mentioned at the beginning of these writings, I have always had a keen interest in prophecy and end-time teachings, much of which have come from the book of Revelation. I have always enjoyed reading Revelation, and I am spurred on to read more of Revelation from the admonition given in Revelation 1:3, *Blessed is the one who reads the words of this prophecy, and blessed are those who hear it and take to heart what is written in it, because the time is near.*

As I read the book of Revelation from my early years as a Christian, sometimes my reading generated more questions than answers. I have always believed that as we approach the time of the Lord's coming, the answers to our questions would be made plain to us. Over the years, I have read many of the classic books on the End Times. But as I look at Revelation in light of what has been happening in the last few years, I am seeing events coming together that make total sense. These events were never thought about thirty years ago when I was only a few years old in the Lord. Thirty years ago, who would have imagined the problems we are having with the Muslim nations and terrorists today? How could we have thought that the Muslim countries would hate America and want to see us destroyed, so that we would not stand in the way of the radical Muslims' ultimate goal of destroying Israel? Today, things are becoming so clear that I believe we need to revisit how we connect the dots to help us understand how the end-times' puzzle fits together.

To start off, I will examine the question: "Could we be wrong about a pre-Tribulation Rapture?" The first thought being: "When does the Great Tribulation start?" This is easy for my discussion, as it seems that many are in agreement that the Great Tribulation begins with the antichrist establishing a seven-year peace treaty with Israel and the Muslim nations, as mentioned in the book of Daniel. This event cannot happen until the antichrist is revealed. I believe the antichrist is revealed close to the opening of the first seal of the seven seals found in chapter six of the book of Revelation.

THE FIRST SIX SEALS IN REVELATION

The opening of the first seal reveals events that will take place close to the beginning of the Great Tribulation. I will show you from God's Word why the events that mark the beginning of the wrath of God will not occur until the trumpet judgments and the bowls of God's wrath later in the Great Tribulation. As I studied for this book, I learned that many believe that the wrath of God starts with the four horses at the opening of the seals. I will address this in greater detail later in this study, showing why I believe that the seals are not part of God's wrath. So for the sake of setting up my later discussion, I will bring you through the opening of the seals.

One reason, which points to the seals as representing events happening during the Great Tribulation that are not the outpouring of God's wrath, is that the fifth seal is the martyrdom of the saints. It is not God doing this to His saints.

A second reason why I do not believe that the opening of the seals represents the wrath of God is that God promised his saints that we would not be accounted for the wrath to come. If you carefully read Revelation 5:2, it says, *And I saw a mighty angel proclaiming in a loud voice, Who is worthy to break the seals and open the scroll? But no one in heaven or on earth or under the earth could open the scroll or even look inside it.* As you read this, you see there was a message in the opening of each seal, but it is inside the <u>scroll</u> that the wrath of God is found. The seals are only the locks that are opened by the Lamb to reveal what is contained inside the scroll.

The Lamb opened the first seal in Revelation 6:1. Here, it talks of a white horse and its rider who held a bow. This is seen as a false Christ coming. I believe this is the revealing of the antichrist. We have seen false Christs for generations, but this one is riding a white horse, imitating Christ. He has a bow, and no arrows are mentioned, for he is only an imitator without the power. My chapter on the coming antichrist is very insightful and will help in understanding this seal.

The second seal is a red horse whose rider is to take peace from the earth. Wars will be happening all over the earth. This will be far worse than wars and rumors of wars. I believe we will see many wars breaking out throughout the earth to mark this event; yet these wars are not the ones to come at the end of the seven-year time of the Great Tribulation. Later, I will discuss some thoughts I have on which nations I believe will be part of this seal.

The third seal talks about a black horse. Its rider will hold a pair of scales and say, *A quart of wheat for a day's wages.* This is talking about global famine, and this famine will result in the starvation of millions. Economists are saying that hyper-inflation and a global economic collapse are coming. It is no longer a question of *if,* but *when* it will hit. It has been said that 2009 was a year of many crop failures in America. In America we are used to having all the food we need just a few minutes away at the local grocery store. In America, we have had our silos full of wheat and other food commodities for years. What I have recently learned is that our back-up reserves have been disappearing, much being sold to China and Russia. China, a country that was once content to live on a bowl of rice, is now expanding their diet as their economy has expanded.

The year 2010 brought even more crop and food failures. A drought in Russia destroyed twenty-five percent of their wheat crops, and they cut off all exports of wheat in 2010. Russia is the world's largest exporter of wheat. When the seals start to open, and food shortages start to emerge, it will cause food panics unlike anything we have ever seen in America. This will lead to rapid inflation and rationing to try to keep food on store shelves. Ultimately, this will lead to a system of rationing that will require us to accept the antichrist's system in order to buy our food.

The fourth seal is Death followed by Hades, revealed as a rider on a pale horse. *And I looked, and behold a pale horse: and his name that sat on him was Death, and Hell followed with him. And power was given unto them over the fourth part of the earth, to kill with sword, and with hunger, and with death, and with the beasts of the earth.* Revelation 6:8 (KJV). I believe that the plagues mentioned here could be the work of terrorists using biological weapons to bring plagues and death to those whom this event is describing. It may also be possible that the plagues could be epidemics from viruses like SARS (severe acute respiratory system) or the swine flu. I have heard some say that this seal will lead to the death of one-quarter of the inhabitants on earth, but if we read this carefully, we realize it is saying that it will affect one-quarter of the earth geographically. It does not say that all will die in this one-quarter of the earth. Later, I will explain which countries could be involved. Three of these countries comprise about one-quarter of the earth's geopraphic area.

The fifth seal talks about Christians who are slain for their testimony of Christ during this part of the Great Tribulation. Read the following from Revelation 6:9-11, *When he opened the fifth seal, I saw under the altar, the souls of those who had been slain because of the word of God and the testimony they had maintained. They called out in a loud voice, How long, Sovereign Lord, holy and true, until you judge the inhabitants of the earth and avenge our blood? Then each of them was given a white robe, and they were told to wait a little longer, until the number of their fellow servants and brothers who were to be killed as they had been, was completed.*

These are interesting verses to think about. These verses reveal that Christians will be killed for staying true to God under the rule of the antichrist. One point to note is that they are under the altar, not at the throne. They are being told to wait for others who are to be killed, for they were to join them. Remember this phrase, "under the altar." It will be important later in this study. Also, note that those who are being killed for their testimony for Christ are asking God, *How long, Sovereign Lord, holy and true, until you judge the inhabitants of the earth and avenge our blood?* They could only ask this question if the wrath of God had not yet started. I will be showing more reasons later that add evidence to why the wrath of God does not start until Revelation, chapter eight.

The sixth seal describes events happening in the heavens with the sun and the moon being affected. Revelation 6:12-17 (KJV) says, *And I beheld when he had opened the sixth seal, and, lo, there was a great earthquake; and the sun became black as sackcloth of hair, and the moon became as blood; And the stars of heaven fell unto the earth, even as a fig tree casteth her untimely figs, when she is shaken of a mighty wind. And the heaven departed as a scroll when it is rolled together; and every mountain and island were moved out of their places. And the kings of the earth, and the great men, and the rich men, and the chief captains, and the mighty men, and every bondman, and every free man, hid themselves in the dens and in the rocks of the mountains; And said to the mountains and rocks, Fall on us, and hide us from the face of him that sitteth on the throne, and from the wrath of the Lamb: For the great day of his wrath is come; and who shall be able to stand?*

This passage explains that the sun will be turned black and the moon will be blood-red. It talks about great earthquakes affecting the whole earth. I will cover this seal in greater detail later in this study. I believe that a cataclysmic event has been waiting to happen that could fulfill this seal.

Now something interesting happens during a break before the seventh seal is opened. In fact, all of chapter seven takes place and it is not until chapter eight that the seventh seal is opened. When the seventh seal is opened at the beginning of chapter eight, it says that when he opened the seal, there was silence in heaven for about half an hour, and the seventh seal was left a mystery.

What I want to do is go back and look at what happened in chapter seven. I have read other writers of prophecy discourse about this being an interlude during which millions of souls would be reached with the Gospel. This is the time the 144,000 Jews will be sealed to go out and take the Gospel and salvation knowledge of Christ to the Jews. I have heard over the years that eventually the time of the Gentiles would be over, and the dispensation for the revealing of Christ to the Jews would begin. At this time, I want to show you some events that are happening in Revelation 7.

The first observation I have made about the events of this chapter is that, if this is the time of the sealing of the 144,000 Jewish evangelists, then would it not make sense this is the beginning of the dispensation of the salvation of the Jews? And would it also make sense that this would be the end of the time of the Gentiles? As I discuss later in this study, I believe a great ingathering of Jews will occur at this time, just before the Rapture of God's elect.

Of course, there can be no credible study of the Rapture or the End Times unless we first thoroughly examine the scriptures. In the next chapter, I want to show you the scriptures that talk about the Rapture. Look at those scriptures from every angle possible, and decide what the Bible really says about the time of the return of Jesus Christ to rapture His saints.

— CHAPTER TWO —
A NEEDED SECOND LOOK
AT THE RAPTURE

Before we offer any thoughts on the time of the Rapture, let's take a look at scripture verses that talk about the Rapture of the believers. It seems to be a consensus among prophetic teachers in the pre-tribulation camp that Revelation 4:1 describes the Rapture.

Revelation 4:1: *After this I looked, and there before me was a door standing open in heaven. And the voice I had first heard speaking to me like a trumpet said, "Come up here, and I will show you what must take place after this."*

Jack Van Impe and many other teachers of a pre-tribulation rapture use this verse to denote the Rapture of the church. Before we look at this verse in depth, I want to show you an event that happens in chapter seven after the sealing of the 144,000 Jews.

Revelation 7:9-12, *After this I looked and there before me was a great multitude that no one could count, from every nation, tribe, people and language, standing before the throne and in front of the Lamb. They were wearing white robes and were holding palm branches in their hands. And they cried out in a loud voice: "Salvation belongs to our God, who sits on the throne, and to the Lamb." All the angels were standing around the throne and around the elders and the four living creatures. They fell down on their faces before the throne and worshiped God, saying, "Amen! Praise and glory and wisdom and thanks and honor and power and strength be to our God for ever and ever, Amen!"*

Look at verse nine. It says, *A great multitude from every nation, tribe, people and language, standing before the throne.* Now go down to verse thirteen and hear what one of the elders who was at the throne has to say. *Then one of the elders asked me, "These in white robes -- who are they, and where did they come from?"*

Now, get the picture? One of the elders, who day and night is around the throne of God, suddenly notices a great multitude of uncountable Christians in white robes standing around the throne worshiping God. He acts as if he did not know where they came from. Then he answers his own question. Listen to the answer in verse fourteen. *I answered, "Sir, you know." And he said, "These are they who have come out of the Great Tribulation; they have washed their robes and made them white in the blood of the Lamb."*

My question is, "If this great multitude just now showed up in heaven after the sixth seal, and the Rapture happened in Revelation 4:1 before the Great Tribulation started, then who are these who just showed up?" Is there a second rapture for the tribulation saints? I do not see that as scriptural. To me, what we are seeing here is the church going through part of the Great Tribulation until it gets to the part where the 144,000 Jews are sealed to be God's chosen messengers to start preaching and revealing the love of Christ to the Jewish nation. I believe the 144,000 Jewish evangelists will bring many Jews to Christ, just in time for the Rapture of the bride of Christ.

One argument I have heard against what I just said is that this is a second rapture for the Jews. A big problem with this explanation is, "Why would you have a separate rapture of the Jews when all Jews who accept Christ will go up in the Rapture anyway?" Besides, the two witnesses who play a part in God's dealing with the Jews are not even yet mentioned. They are to witness to the Jewish nation for three and a half years during the second half of the Great Tribulation. So how can Revelation 7:14 be about a second rapture of the Jews? Also, when you read Revelation 7:9, it says these people who have just appeared in heaven came from every nation, tribe, people, and language.

The same argument is used that these are <u>Jews</u> who are living in every nation and speaking in every language. However, this verse says, "Every people, nation and language." This verse ties into another, and the result is very exciting. Look at Revelation 5:9. This scripture reveals that only Jesus was qualified to open the seals. *You are worthy to take the scroll and to open its seals, because you were slain, and with your blood you purchased men for God from every tribe, language, people, and nation.* THIS IS ME AND YOU! THIS IS THE CHURCH THAT CHRIST REDEEMED WITH HIS BLOOD. Now look at Revelation 7:9 and you will see Christ collecting in the Rapture what he has already purchased! *After this I looked, and there before me was a great multitude that no one could count, from every NATION, TRIBE, PEOPLE, and LANGUAGE, standing before the throne and in front of the Lamb.*

Please pay close attention to what I am going to show you.

I want to take you back to an event that lies between Revelation 4:1 and Revelation 7:11-14. Remember, Revelation 4:1 is the pre-tribulation verse for the occurrence of the Rapture. Look at Revelation 5:11-12 (KJV): *And I beheld, and I heard the voice of many angels around the throne and the beasts and the elders: and the number of them was ten thousand times ten thousand and thousands of thousands; Saying with a loud voice, "Worthy is the Lamb that was slain to receive power and riches and wisdom and strength, and honor and glory and blessing."* **Look at who are described as being around the throne. It is angels, beasts, and elders, but there is no mention of <u>saints</u> around the throne. If the saints were raptured in Revelation 4:1, they would be around the throne in white robes in this passage.**

Now when you read Revelation 7:11-14, you hear the elder, who is always around the throne, asking, "Who are these multitudes that no one can number in white robes...?" Who are these people that have suddenly shown up? The elder then reflects, and he says that they are those who have come out of the Great Tribulation. **Now stop right here and think about this. If the Rapture had already happened pre-tribulation in Revelation 4:1, then the millions of pre-tribulation Christians would have been in white robes around the throne in both Revelation chapter five and chapter seven. They would have blended in with the multitude that the elder was asking about in Revelation 7:11-14. Do you think there are two raptures? No. I do not see this in the Word of God. These verses show the Rapture just did not happen until Revelation 7:9.**

Next, I would like to go to 1 Thessalonians 4:15-18. This scripture shows why the Rapture could not have happened until after Revelation 5:11-12. Read 1 Thessalonians 4:15-18 (KJV): *For this we say unto you by the word of the Lord, that we which are alive and remain unto the coming of the Lord shall not prevent them which are asleep. For the Lord himself shall descend from heaven with a shout, with the voice of the archangel, and with the trump of God: and the dead in Christ will rise first: Then we which are alive and remain shall be caught up together with them in the clouds, to meet the Lord in the air:* ***and so shall we ever be with the Lord****. Wherefore comfort one another with these words.*

This scripture shows why the Rapture could not have happened until after Revelation 5:11-12. Read 1 Thessalonians 4:17 again. It says that both the dead in Christ and those who are alive will both be raptured together to meet the Lord in the air, and then it says that we shall ever be with the Lord. If, from the point of the Rapture, we will forever be with the Lord, then think about this. If we will be with the Lord, then we would have been with the Lord in Revelation 5:11-12 around the throne. But if there is no mention of saints in white robes around the throne in Revelation 5:11-12, the Rapture has not yet happened. So when the elder in Revelation 7:9 and 13 asks who the multitudes in white robes are, whom no man can number, he is told that they are the saints who have come out of the Great Tribulation. Revelation 7:9, *After this I looked and there before me was a great multitude that no one could count, from every nation, tribe, people, and language standing before the throne and in front of the Lamb. They were holding palm branches in their hands.* Can it be any clearer? The Rapture, the only Rapture, has just taken place according to Revelation 7:9.

MARTYRED SAINTS SHOW THE TIMING OF THE RAPTURE

One argument I get is that these saints who suddenly appeared around the throne are martyred saints who are coming out of the Great Tribulation as they are being killed for refusing to take the mark of the beast. I want you to think about this as I share why this could not be the case. To begin with, this event around the throne happens in an instant, proven by the fact that the elder who is asking the question is always at the throne. It is like he blinked, and suddenly there were millions in white robes around the throne. This would mean, if they were the Great Tribulation martyred saints, they would have had to be killed at the same time. I do not think this is possible. Also, there is a second problem with this opinion. When the saints are being martyred, as described in the fifth seal in Revelation 6:9, it says the martyred saints are under the altar and not at the throne. Also, they are asking in, Revelation 6:10-11, *"How long, Sovereign Lord, holy and true, until you judge the inhabitants of the earth and avenge our blood?" Then each of them was given a white robe, and they were told to wait a little longer, until the number of their fellow servants and brothers who were to be killed as they had been was completed.*

The next scripture says they were each given a white robe. Notice, they are still under the altar, not at the throne! If these martyred saints were at the throne in Revelation 6:10, in the white robes that they were given while under the altar, then the elder in Revelation 7 would not have even noticed a second multitude showing up. For over 2000 years, millions of Christians have been martyred. At the point of the Rapture, they would all have <u>been</u> at the throne. **Now think about this: if all the martyred saints of all time do not show up at the throne until Revelation 7:9, then how can we say the Rapture happened in**

Revelation 4:1?

Now let us go back and look at Revelation 4:1, which is considered the pre-tribulation rapture verse. *After this I looked, and there before me was a door standing open in heaven. And the voice I had first heard speaking to me like a trumpet said, "Come up here, and I will show you what must take place after this." At once I was in the Spirit, and there before me was the throne in heaven with someone sitting on it.*

I just do not see the Rapture in Revelation 4:1. What I do see is John, the Revelator, being taken to heaven to the very throne of God where God tells him, *...I will show you what must take place after this.* Paul had a similar experience when Christ was disclosing revelations to him. Then, if you will go to Revelation 19:11, you will see the heavens opened up again, just like what happened in Revelation 4:1. Read Revelation 19:11: *I saw heaven standing open, and there before me was a white horse, whose rider is called Faithful and True. With justice he judges and makes war.* This is a revelation of Christ after the battles have been won, and the marriage supper of the Lamb is about to take place. This heaven standing open does not mean a gateway is open for a rapture event because, if you will go back to Revelation 19:6-8, you will see that the saints are already <u>in</u> heaven about to celebrate with Christ at the marriage supper of the Lamb. Read Revelation 19:6-8, *Then I heard what sounded like a great multitude, like the roar of rushing waters, and like loud peals of thunder, shouting: "Hallelujah! For our Lord God Almighty reigns. Let us rejoice and be glad and give him glory! For the wedding of the Lamb has come, and his bride has made herself ready. Fine linen, bright and clean, was given her to wear."*

I would like to know where there is a second or third scripture that shows the timing of the Rapture as being pre-tribulation. I was taught in Bible school that doctrine has to be backed with the witness of two or three scriptures. You might ask where I see two or more scriptures to support the Rapture as happening after the opening of the six seals in Revelation 6. I have already shown you a number of verses in

Revelation that show the Rapture happening after the opening of the seals during the Great Tribulation. Now I want to show you from the Gospels where I see three places that describe almost verbatim what is happening in the opening of the seven seals of Revelation 6. All three describe what I believe is the Rapture, happening after the opening of the sixth seal.

Please read the following verses:

Matthew 24:4-5: *Jesus answered: "Watch out that no one deceives you. For many will come in my name claiming, 'I am the Christ', and will deceive many."* This verse coincides with the first seal about false christs.

Matthew 24:7a: *Nation will rise against nation, and kingdom against kingdom.* This coincides with the second seal.

Matthew 24:7b: *There will be famines and earthquakes in various places.* This coincides with the third seal.

Matthew 24:9: *Then you will be handed over to be persecuted and put to death, and you will be hated by all nations because of me.* This coincides with the fifth seal.

Matthew 24:29: *The sun will be darkened, and the moon will not give its light, the stars will fall from the sky, and the heavenly bodies will be shaken.* This coincides with the sixth seal.

Now read Matthew 24:30-31, ***At that time****, the sign of the Son of Man will appear in the sky, and all the nations of the earth will mourn. They will see the Son of Man coming on the clouds of the sky, with power and great glory. And he will send his angels with a loud trumpet call, and they will gather his elect from the four winds, from one end of the heavens to the other.* Am I taking this wrong? I do not think so. This sounds like the Rapture. Look at Mark 13:6-27, and you will see a similar parallel. Then look at Luke 21:8-27, and you will see another.

One of the established arguments for the pre-tribulation rapture is conjecture from Revelation 4:1. Some teachers are saying that the church is not mentioned after Revelation 4:1. I do not see this as true, for it says the saints would be martyred during the fifth seal of the Great Tribulation in Revelation 6. Again, Revelation 14:11-13 is about those who are taking the mark of the beast and the necessity of patience for the saints. During this time, it goes on to say, many saints will be martyred. Now I know there are some who teach that these are tribulation saints. Tell me, where are the words "tribulation saints" found in the Bible?

Realize, we are setting the time of the Rapture as a pre-tribulation event, not based on scripture verses, but based on the omission of the word "church" after Revelation 4:1. As I see it, the timing of the Rapture is too important to establish this doctrine without scripture, chapter, and verse to back up this position. **Plus, think about this: what is the church? It is the saints that make the church, so if the saints are mentioned after Revelation 4:1, then the church is mentioned. Later in chapter nine, I do a study on the church, and what I found really strengthens what I am saying here.**

In closing, I want to pose the question that some will ask, "Is it really that important when the Rapture happens? Shouldn't we just be ready?" This is a good question. The problem I see is, if the churches are teaching that the Rapture will come before the Great Tribulation, then this gives the church a false sense of security. I have heard pastors say God would not allow His church to go through suffering. Yet as I mentioned above in Revelation 14:11-13, it says that the saints will have to have patient endurance during the Great Tribulation when the antichrist is pushing his system of the mark of the beast. If the saints who have expected the pre-tribulation Rapture are suddenly seeing themselves in the Great Tribulation without warning and no time to get ready for this turbulent time, I believe it will cause many Christians to turn away from God. They may start believing that they have been abandoned by God, and I believe it will lead to many accepting the system of the antichrist rather than starve to death. I believe that the events happening today, with the world economies on the verge of collapse, are setting the stage to cause the world populations to look for a savior in the form of the antichrist. We, as believers, need to be the ones who are looking for the signs of Christ's coming and preparing for the tribulation of these times as Joseph did in his time. When the hard times come, we will be able to take care of the needs of our families and others. We will be in a position to be used by God for the greatest revival the world has ever seen.

Before moving to the next section, I want to add some thoughts that will answer questions I often hear when this Bible verse is referenced: 1 Thessalonians 1:10 (KJV): *Even Jesus, which delivered us from the wrath to come.* This text is often taken to mean that the Rapture of the church will be a pre-tribulation event in order to spare the church from the wrath of the Great Tribulation, but the Bible calls the time period leading up to the return of Christ "the Great Tribulation," a seven-year period that will become more and more intense as we get closer to Christ's return.

If you look at the beginning of the Great Tribulation and the opening of the seven seals, you will see events that are similar to what has happened for all of time: wars, earthquakes, and famine, and even the martyrdom of the saints, which is the fifth seal. Just like a woman's labor pains grow in intensity as the time of the delivery of her child approaches, it will be the same growth of intensity when the seals are opened at the beginning of the Great Tribulation. The intensity of wars will be higher, earthquakes will be more devastating, and famines will be more widespread.

Most Christians, who hold to the pre-tribulation Rapture believe we will miss out on the seals and all of the Great Tribulation. Many people refer to 1 Thessalonians 1:10 (KJV): *And to wait for his Son from heaven, whom he raised from the dead, even Jesus, which delivered us from the wrath to come.* If you look closely at this verse, it says that we will be delivered from the wrath to come. This means the "wrath of God." This verse does not say that we will be delivered from tribulation to come. In fact, think about it, the Great Tribulation is not called the Great Wrath of God. When the seals are being opened, I do not see the evidence in God's Word that shows the seals are the wrath of God. God does not start wars, create famine, or martyr His saints as described in the fifth seal. The wrath of God does not start until Revelation 8-9, and then it picks up again in chapter fifteen.

We need to understand what the Bible teaches about tribulation. The Bible says tribulation works patience. It is interesting that during the Great Tribulation when the saints are battling with the antichrist, God's Word tells us in Revelation 13:10, *If anyone is to go into captivity, into captivity he will go. If anyone is to be killed with the sword, he will be killed. This calls for patient endurance on the part of the saints.* I believe this passage is teaching us that the saints will be going through a period of tribulation that will lead to a great revival and at the same time bring about a purification of the church. Does the Bible not teach us that Christ is coming back for a pure bride worthy of being called the bride of Christ?

Many churches today are caught up in entertaining both the saved and the lost, believing that great performances will make people feel good and so draw them closer to God. I believe if we would put more effort into ministering to the needs of the hurting, we would see a greater maturity in our churches and a greater harvest of the lost.

I have been reading a book on the Azusa Street Revival called *Azusa Street, They Told Me Their Stories.* I believe this was the greatest revival in the last hundred years. It was a 24/7 prayer meeting. It did not have great entertainers. It didn't even have great preachers. But the Glory of God was there. A cloud, like what appeared in the Old Testament called the Shekinah Glory, would appear. Witnesses said it was like basking in the breath of God, or like being swallowed in God's presence. Miracles were happening as God's servants reached out and prayed for those in need of a miracle. Arms grew back, legs grew back. I don't mean adding a couple of inches; I mean whole arms and legs grew back all the way to the finger nails. One man could hardly make enough of a living to buy food, but when God grew back his arm, his boss rehired him, and this man came back to the revival with two hundred people. Many received miracles that night. A crowd from a deaf school came, and they were all healed. In 1910, it was prophesied by two of the leaders, William Seymour and Charles Parham, that the Shekinah Glory would return and a revival greater then Azusa would come in about one hundred years. This prophecy was made at the end of the Azusa Street Revival in 1910. This revival is due; I believe the revival will come when the time of Christ's coming brings the church back to its knees.

The Bible teaches us that in these last days we will see the birth pains increasing preceding Christ's coming. His coming will turn people's lives upside down. As God allows economic and natural disasters on the earth, Christians may ask, "What are you doing, God?" I imagine God's answer to this question would be, "I'm not trying to make you feel good. I'm trying to wake you up and draw you closer to Me."

I was recently reading a book, *The Best of A. W. Tozer*. He was a great preacher of a previous generation, and he made a profound statement in the chapter, "Why We are Lukewarm About Christ's Return":

"History reveals that times of suffering for the church have also been times of looking upward. Tribulation has always sobered God's people and encouraged them to look for and yearn after the return of the Lord. Our present preoccupation with this world may be a warning of bitter days to come. God will wean us from the earth someway—the easy way if possible, the hard way if necessary. It's up to us."

— CHAPTER THREE —

THE SEALING OF THE 144,000
AND OTHER PRE-RAPTURE EVENTS

As I studied the book of Revelation, I noticed that the 144,000 Jews were mentioned in chapter seven and again in chapter fourteen. In chapter seven, the sealing of these Jews happens just before what I am convinced is the time of the Rapture of the church. As it says in Revelation 7:9, *After this, I looked and there before me was a great multitude that no one could count...* In Revelation 14, the 144,000 are mentioned again, and as we continue reading Revelation 14:14-19, we see what appears to be Jesus Christ in the clouds. Then in Revelation 14:15, the angel tells Jesus Christ to take his sickle and reap the harvest, for he says that the harvest of the earth is ripe. Read on in Revelation 14:16. It says that the earth was harvested. When I read this, it sounded like another description of the Rapture that happened in Revelation 7:9-10.

Matthew 24:30-31 gives another description of the Rapture that sounds very similar to Revelation 14:16. The Matthew passage says, *At that time the sign of the Son of Man will appear in the sky and all the nations of the earth will mourn. They will see the Son of Man coming on the clouds of the sky, with power and great glory. And he will send his angels with a loud trumpet call, and they will gather his elect from the four winds, from one end of the heavens to the other.* Continuing to read in

Revelation 14:17-19, the scripture mentions a second harvest of the earth, harvested and thrown into the winepress of God's wrath. When we go back to the time of the Rapture as described in Revelation 7, we will see that the wrath of God starts in Revelation 8 and 9. When I first discovered this, I figured that Revelation 7 and 14 were two places in Revelation that covered the same event, basically showing that not all of Revelation is in chronological order. This thought made sense to me until I pondered further and eventually got stumped as I studied the 144,000 mentioned in Revelation 14.

As I read Revelation 14:3, *And they sang a new song before the throne,* this really confused me, for this was showing that the 144,000 were with Christ around the throne, <u>before</u> the Rapture described in Revelation 14:14. It really did not seem possible that these Jews would be with Christ around the throne before the Rapture because this would contradict Revelation 9:4!

The Revelation 9:4 passage describes the fifth trumpet of God's wrath when the scorpion-like locusts are instructed not to harm the grass or trees but only those who did not have the mark of God on their foreheads. This passage shows the 144,000 Jews on the earth during the wrath of God, but they are not being harmed by God's wrath. So, you see why I was confused to see these Jews at the throne before the Rapture as described in Revelation 14:14.

I asked God in prayer to please show me why this seemed so confusing. I reread Revelation chapters 7-14 several times. On the third reading, it was like a light bulb came on, and I saw two separate verses that opened these chapters to a much clearer understanding. In fact, I was so excited I could hardly contain it.

If we go back and read about the seven seals, beginning in Revelation 6, we will notice an interlude between the sixth and seventh seals. This interlude in chapter seven is where the 144,000 are sealed, and then the Rapture is described. Next, when we read Revelation 8, the seventh seal is opened, and the seven trumpets of God's wrath start to sound.

These trumpets continue through the sounding of the sixth trumpet of God's wrath at the end of Revelation 9. Then there is another interruption just before the sounding of the seventh trumpet of God's wrath. During this interruption, a few different events in Revelation 10 and the first half of Revelation 11 are described. It is in this section I saw the first key to understanding why I was confused with the second description of the 144,000 Jews in Revelation 14.

If you read Revelation 10, you will see that during this interruption, a second, smaller scroll is opened and read by John the Revelator. After John read the scroll, he was told in Revelation 10:11, *Then I was told, "You must prophesy again about many peoples, nations, languages, and kings."* What is happening here is John, the writer of Revelation, is being told to prophesy again about the people who suddenly appear around the throne in Revelation 7:9. These are the same ones who, I believe, were the raptured and martyred saints which the elder was asking about in Revelation 7. So from Revelation 10:11 until the second description of the Rapture that is referred to as the harvest of the earth in Revelation 14:9, John is given further insights into a number of events.

These chapters, Revelation 10:11-14:2, contain some events that are pre-rapture events and show that this section of Revelation is not chronologically in order. Shortly, I will go into more detail about some of the events mentioned here. These chapters contain some exciting events that will take place before the Rapture, as described in both Revelation 7 and 14.

First, I want to show you how I understood there is no contradiction concerning the 144,000 Jews who were described as being around the throne with Jesus in Revelation 14. Revelation 14:1 says, *Then I looked and there before me was the Lamb, standing on Mount Zion and with him 144,000 who had his name and his Father's name written on their foreheads.* The key is that the Lamb is standing on Mount Zion. This event does not take place until Jesus returns to the earth at the end of the Great Tribulation. These verses confirm that some of these events in Revelation 10:11 through Revelation 14 are not in chronological order.

While meditating on these verses describing the 144,000, I noticed a verse that posed another dilemma. Revelation 14:4 says, *They were purchased from among men and offered as first-fruits to God and the Lamb.* The problem I noticed in this verse was that they are described as being offered to God and the Lamb as first-fruits. This term, first-fruits, is often seen as a reference to the first-fruits of the resurrection. How can the 144,000 Jews sealed in Revelation 7 be the first-fruits of the resurrection when the saints are raptured before these Jews get resurrected bodies at the end of the Great Tribulation? One logical explanation I see is when the 144,000 are sealed to do God's mission on earth throughout the time of God's wrath, they could be given their resurrected bodies. When they are sealed and receive resurrected bodies in Revelation 7, they would be the first-fruits of the resurrection <u>before</u> the Rapture of the saints takes place in Revelation 7:9. This explanation answers many questions about the 144,000 Jews who are chosen to do a special mission for God.

When you read Revelation 9:4, about how the scorpion locusts are unable to harm the 144,000, it would make sense they could not be harmed if they have resurrected bodies. Many teachers say the mission of the144,000 is to be evangelists to the Jews around the world and to point the Jews to Jesus as the Messiah who first came 2,000 years ago. The Jews did not recognize Christ the first time. Think about this: these 144,000 Jews appear on the scene just before the Rapture as described in Revelation 7:9. This is the time when the antichrist is waging war against the saints; then when the two witnesses appear, the antichrist wages war against the saints. But nowhere does it say that Satan or the antichrist is waging war against the 144,000 chosen Jews. If they were given their resurrected bodies at the time they are sealed, then Satan could not touch them as they are no longer living in a mortal body. Here is another thought that reinforces this explanation. These sealed Jews have a daunting task. They have to go throughout the world during this time when the antichrist will have them marked as terrorists. It will not be easy for them to travel freely, let alone be able to make it through airport security with a mark on their foreheads, telling everyone that they are special emissaries sent from God.

If they have been given their resurrected bodies, they will be able to get their assignments supernaturally from God and will be able to travel supernaturally as Christ did when He came back to the earth with His resurrected body. This allowed Jesus to appear and disappear or walk through walls. So, if the 144,000 specially chosen Jews will be able to move freely and instantly to whatever destination God sends them to without any fear of harm from the antichrist or man, they will accomplish God's will to reach the Jews scattered throughout the world in record time.

Now think about this. If it makes sense that the 144,000 Jews are sealed and given resurrected bodies in Revelation 7, and they are the first-fruits of the Resurrection, then how can the Rapture of the church be Revelation 4:1? The saints and the 144,000 Jews cannot both be the first-fruits. **Also think about this: first-fruits denotes a small portion of the harvest, before the full harvest takes place. It makes more sense that the 144,000 are first-fruits (a portion of the harvest) than the harvest of the saints that cannot be numbered in Revelation 7:9. Also, realize the 144,000 cannot be the first-fruits if the Rapture happened in Revelation 4:1.**

I said earlier I would cover some of the events contained in these chapters in Revelation that John the Revelator was instructed to prophesy again, concerning the peoples to be raptured. I believe the section that contains these events is from the beginning of Revelation 11 to the second description of the Rapture in Revelation 14:14. This section is out of chronological order. Some of these events covered here go back before the Rapture, and some events go forward to when Christ physically returns to the earth and stands on Mt. Zion. Some events occur between these two.

The first event I believe John was prophesying about, which would have a connection to the people who would be raptured, concerns the two witnesses. The two witnesses are on the earth for three and one-half years. If they are killed by the antichrist before the end of the seven years of the Great Tribulation, then this means that they appear at some point before the middle of the seven years. This makes it possible, if the Rapture happens at some point close to the middle of the seven years, for the saints to witness the appearing of the two witnesses before the Rapture. To me, this is very exciting, for this will be another supernatural event God will send to the earth to show those who are lost that Jesus is coming soon and wants to attract as many as possible to Himself before the Rapture. As I study Revelation 12 and 13, there is so much to grasp for each piece of the prophetic puzzle to fit together. I believe some of the prophecies here will not be fully understood until future events begin to unfold.

In conclusion to this section of my study, I would like to point out an event I believe we will witness before the Rapture. This portion of my study is found in Revelation 14 before it talks about the harvest of the earth mentioned in Revelation 14:14, which I believe is a second description of the Rapture. Revelation 14:6-11 covers the coming of three angels sent by God to bring a message to the world. If we reread Revelation 7:1-2, we will read about four angels on the earth. Then it says in Revelation 7:2, *Then I saw another angel coming up from the east, having the seal of the living God...* This angel goes on to call the other four angels to help him put the seal of the living God on the 144,000 Jews. Read Revelation 7:3: *Do not harm the land or the sea or the trees until WE put the seal on the foreheads of the servants of our God.*

If we read this portion carefully, we realize these angels who are asked to help seal the 144,000 Jews are the ones who will deliver the wrath of God, but they have been asked to hold off until some point after the sealing of the 144,000 Jews. **This is another key scripture pointing out that the wrath of God does not start until some point after the sealing of the 144,000.**

Another interesting observation is there will be many angels involved during this seven-year period. When we read Revelation 14:6, the same phrase is used: *Then I saw another angel flying in midair...* This angel has a mission to those living on the earth. Read Revelation 14:6-7, *Then I saw another angel flying in midair, and he had the eternal gospel to proclaim to those who live on the earth - to every nation, tribe, language, and people. He said in a loud voice. "Fear God and give him glory, because the hour of his judgment has come. Worship him who made the heavens, the earth, the sea and the springs of water."* It is so exciting that this angel is sent to proclaim the gospel to those who live on the earth.

Going into detail, the angel describes the people he is speaking to in the same terms as those who will be involved in the Rapture later in Revelation 14:6-7 as the people from every nation, tribe, language, and people. He is speaking again of the Gentiles who are eligible for the Rapture. As we read further, the angel proclaims what man is to do before the judgment of God begins, for it says, *Fear God and give him glory, because the hour of his judgment has come.* This verse is important to understand.

What I have been showing is these chapters are not in chronological order. As you see, it says the hour of His judgment has come. But when you read Revelation 8 and 9, the judgment or the wrath of God starts after what I see as the Rapture in chapter seven. This is illustrated with the warning from the first of three angels for the nations to repent before the wrath of God to come, as described in the second description of the Rapture in Revelation 14.

Therefore, the first angel is given the mission of helping the saints to bring in the last part of the harvest before the Rapture happens, and the wrath of God begins. **There are not two raptures but rather two accounts describing the same event with God's wrath following.**

Next, Revelation 14:8 goes on to talk about the second angel: *A second angel followed and said, "Fallen! Fallen is Babylon the Great, which made all nations drink the maddening wine of her adulteries."* I believe that

Babylon the Great which will fall is America. I go into this in greater detail later in this study. I believe when it says Babylon the Great has fallen, it is referring to governmental, social, and economic collapse, not the full destruction of Babylon that is to come later as described in Revelation 18.

I believe this collapse could be triggered by several possible events. One possible choice would be that we would be destroyed by our enemies. Another could be the catastrophic event described in the sixth seal of Revelation. I go into this event in greater detail later in my chapter called "The Window of the Lord's Return." This event would bring America to a new low.

Next, Revelation 14:9 talks about the third angel following the first two, and the wording conveys that the three angels will appear in chronological order. The third angel is proclaiming the judgment of God and the eternal punishment about to come on those who fail to heed this message. At a time when the church will be under great persecution and will have moved underground to avoid the oppression of the antichrist, these angels will move about openly proclaiming the gospel. This will take away any excuse that man would have about knowing God's plan of redemption.

As you read these verses in Revelation 14:9-12, you will see that the mark of the beast is being forced on the world at this time. Christians and all who do not want to come under God's judgment must at all costs refuse this mark and the system of the antichrist. Remember, the wording of the three angels shows this is chronological; verse twelve is a message to the saints. It is telling the saints that this will be a trying time, but we must remain faithful to Jesus, as the rewards are great.

The next verse confirms there will be trying times, and we must be faithful at all costs. Hebrews 10:35-38 states, *So do not throw away your confidence; it will be richly rewarded. You need to persevere so that when you have done the will of God, you will receive what he has promised. For in just a little while, he who is coming will come and will not delay. But my righteous ones will live by faith. And if he shrinks back, I will not be pleased with him.*

Read Revelation 14:9-12. *A third angel followed them and said in a loud voice: "If anyone worships the beast and his image and receives his mark on the forehead or on the hand, he too, will drink of the wine of the wrath of God's fury, which has been poured full strength into the cup of his wrath. He will be tormented with burning sulfur in the presence of the holy angels and of the Lamb. And the smoke of their torment rises forever and ever.* **There is no rest day or night for those who worship the beast and his image, or for anyone who receives the mark of his name."** *This calls for the patient endurance on the part of the saints who obey God's commandments and remain faithful to Jesus.*

As we approach the coming of the Lord, we will be facing challenging times. Many Christians are fearful they will have to go through any part of the Great Tribulation. Some Christians wonder how a loving God could allow His people to go through any of this tribulation.

I believe we must have the same resolve to serve God as the saints of the early church had. They were not just willing to live for God; they were willing to die for God. This was not as a way of obtaining grace and salvation. It was because they already had God's grace and salvation. Look at what happened to the disciples who were first imprisoned and then released by an angel. When they were brought before the religious leaders who wanted to kill them, listen to the attitude of these early believers who were experiencing trials and persecution. Acts 5:40-41 says, ... *They called the apostles in and had them flogged. Then they ordered them not to speak in the name of Jesus and let them go. The apostles left the Sanhedrin, rejoicing, because they had been counted worthy of suffering disgrace for the Name.*

Look at what happened in China when Mao took over; he had thousands of Christians killed. The 80,000 Christians in China had to go underground, but did they give up their faith? No! The church oppressed with tribulation and persecution in China grew from 80,000 to somewhere between 100 to 200 million Christians today. We are God's army, and we must recognize that as we get closer to the Lord's return, Satan will be ramping up his attack on the earth to keep people from getting saved.

It just does not make sense that God would take the saints out before the harvest is complete. Read 2 Peter 3:9, *The Lord is not slow in keeping his promise, as some understand slowness. He is patient with you, not wanting anyone to perish, but everyone to come to repentance.*

If God is so determined to bring the lost to Himself that He would send angels to help in the last days before His return, does it not make sense that God would leave His army here to lead the lost to Christ until the last minute and THEN rapture his saints off the earth just before He pours out His wrath and judgment on those who have rejected Him?

CHAPTER FOUR

HOW DOES THE UNITED STATES FIT INTO THE PROPHETIC PICTURE?

T his is a question that has intrigued me forever. The Bible does not address the United States in plain-speak, so you have to wonder how do we fit into all of this? I guess an easy answer would be that we just become absorbed into and under the rule of the antichrist. Our Constitution is cancelled, and the USA becomes irrelevant as we know it. **I was told by one pastor that it might be that the United States will be left out of the events concerning the antichrist and the mark of the beast altogether. Do not hold your breath on that hope. That is truly wishful thinking. Do you really think that Satan, indwelling a world leader who has designs to rule the planet forever, would think of leaving America as a Christian nation to be free to do its own thing? To fully dispel this thought, read Revelation 13:7** *He was given power to make war against the saints and to conquer them. And he was given authority over EVERY tribe, people, language, and NATION.* **America is a nation.**

Over the years, my thoughts on this subject have led me to see that we have been the main protector of Israel, thus causing the United States to be standing in the way of many of the prophetic events that have to fall into place. As long as the United States is a strong superpower, we would not stand by and let Israel be attacked and destroyed, for we have always provided them with armaments and supplies. The early thoughts I had were as follows:

1) We would be defeated in a world war, and we would not be around to do any more protecting.

2) The United States would have an economic collapse which would make us so poor that we could no longer hold the position as Israel's protector and as the world cop. Also, our problems would be so severe at home that we would need all our military and police forces to keep things under control at home, resulting in a deficit of resources for dealing with world problems any more. This is difficult to envision and I do not want to see these kinds of hard times. I certainly do not want to experience an event like the Great Depression of the thirties that hit my father's generation, but I have always believed that for the end-time events to unfold, according to that which has been laid out in the Bible, then America and the world would have to experience a widespread economic collapse.

3) My next thought is a long one and the most thought provoking. I have questioned the scriptures I am about to share with you, wondering for years if they could be talking about the United States. If it were not for the fact that I have read other prophetic writers sharing my questions and possible conclusions, I would hesitate to share these thoughts

Where do we begin? If you read Revelation 18 about the destruction of "Mystery Babylon," you have to wonder if America could be a spiritual type of the actual, physical and geographically-located Babylon. Most Bible teachers believe these scriptures are talking about Iraq. But when you carefully read the passage, you will see many scripture verses that show the country of Iraq does not fit the description of the country to be destroyed in judgment

Here is an example: Revelation 18:10 says, *Woe! Woe! O great city, O Babylon, city of power! In one hour your doom has come!* **Iraq is not a**

city of power today; they had their day, and so the question I have is whether these scriptures are talking about a country that has the spirit of Babylon rather than the geographic location of Iraq. If you read these scriptures with that thought in mind and apply the thought that the city of power being referred to is the United States, then see if it makes sense to you.

For example, read Revelation 17:1-2: *...Come, I will show you the punishment of the great prostitute, who sits on many waters. With her the kings of the earth committed adultery and the inhabitants of the earth were intoxicated with the wine of her adulteries.* Geographically, the United States sits on many waters and contains many peoples from many nationalities, and Iraq does not. Now read Revelation 17:15, *The waters you saw, where the prostitute sits are peoples, multitudes, nations and languages.* America is a land known as a land of many peoples and languages, and Iraq is not. Revelation 17:18 says, *The woman you saw is the great city that rules over the kings of the earth.* This sounds like the United States, not Iraq

Revelation 18:1-3 talks about the fall of this great city and Revelation 18:4 says, *Come out of her, my people.* I have been doing a bit of a study on this verse, focusing on the two words "my people;" at first, I thought it referred to Christians. Now I see the strong possibility it is addressing the Jews as God's chosen people. In 2 Chronicles 7:14 it says, *If my people who are called by my name will humble themselves and pray and seek my face and turn from their wicked ways, then will I hear from heaven and will forgive their sin and heal their land.* This verse is God speaking to His people, the Jews, in answer to their prayers when they were praying to God during the dedication of the temple. This phrase, "my people," is most often used to refer to God's chosen people, the Jews. If you look at Romans 9:25, you will see it can also mean the Gentiles who have been accepted as God's people because of Christ's sacrifice on the cross. Romans 9:25: *...I will call them 'my people' who are not my people; and I will call her 'my loved one' who is not my loved one.* When you study Revelation, you will see the Christians are spoken about collectively as the church or referred to as saints. It is my conclusion the reference to "my people" in Revelation 18:4 is speaking to the Jews after the Rapture has taken place. I will go into greater detail in the next chapter entitled, "God's No Man Left Behind."

As we continue to look at the possibility that "Mystery Babylon" is going to be destroyed, it can seem a bit unnerving and depressing. I have to point out that if we are talking about the total destruction of America, we can rejoice that before its destruction, God will evacuate His people before He lets loose His wrath of destruction. Read Revelation 18:17-18. *In one hour, such great wealth has been brought to ruin! Every sea captain, and all who travel by ship, the sailors and all who earn their living from the sea, will stand far off, when they see the smoke of her burning, they will exclaim, "Was there ever a city like this great city?"* Does this sound like Iraq or the United States? Also, ask yourself, "What other country could this chapter be talking about?" Well, any Bible scholar would eliminate Russia and China. It would not be Europe, as this is the center of the antichrist's rule, and the revived Roman Empire is the country that is ready to destroy Mystery Babylon. Some say Mystery Babylon is Rome, ruled by the Pope. I do not see this as a land of commerce over which the merchants of the world would mourn. Could it be a Middle Eastern country like Iraq? I would have to say no for two reasons. First, the description of this country just does not fit any of the countries of the Middle East, and the Bible says the antichrist wants to ultimately destroy Israel. If the Middle Eastern countries want Israel destroyed, then this makes these countries friends of the antichrist. I am sorry; I just do not see any choice but to say this is describing the fall of the United States. This country is described as "Mystery Babylon." Think about this: the United States is the only superpower today that did not exist when the Bible was written. If the country that is being described did exist during the writing of Revelation, then would it be a mystery?

If you were to ask, "Does the Bible really tell us who God would use to destroy the country we are talking about?" The answer lies in Revelation 17:16. *The beast and the ten horns you saw will hate the prostitute. They will bring her to ruin, and leave her naked; they will eat her flesh and burn her with fire.*

Now after hearing about the fall of the dollar, the rise of the euro, and the choosing of a permanent European leader, it gets easier to see what this verse in Revelation is talking about. I believe "Mystery Babylon" is America, based on my discussion above about the fall of "Mystery Babylon" spoken about in Revelation 18. The leaders behind the new revived Roman Empire and the antichrist will not want to see the US dollar rise again and certainly will not want to see the United States rise to world power again.

An update now shows us that the United States, under the leadership of those who do not support Israel, will pull back our support and ultimately let Israel stand on its own without any outside help.

In concluding this chapter, let it be fully realized that Israel will never be left alone without protection. When it looks like Israel is without allies, the armies of God will be encamped around Israel, and Israel will never be destroyed.

— CHAPTER FIVE —

GOD'S "NO MAN LEFT BEHIND"

I f this study has given you some second thoughts, as it has me, that the Rapture does not happen until Revelation 7, then maybe you will also be convinced that we will not see the Rapture until after the sealing of the 144,000 Jews. This is explained in Revelation 7:3-8. Now read Revelation 7:9 (NIV): *After this, I looked and there before me was a great multitude that no one could count, from every nation, tribe, and people and language, standing before the throne and in front of the Lamb. They were wearing white robes and were holding palm branches in their hands.* I believe this is the rapture as seen from the throne in heaven. After we meet the Lord in the clouds, our Savior will lead us to His home and throne where we will worship God and our Lord and Savior Jesus Christ.

Revelation 8 prophesies of seven angels who hold the seven trumpets of God's wrath that is about to be poured out on the earth. You realize how God manifests His grace to His saints by rescuing them from the earth just before the out-pouring of His wrath.

Going back to the sealing of the 144,000 Jews, there is an important sequence in this event. These Jews are sealed in Revelation 7:1-8. Then at some point after the sealing, the Rapture of the saints takes place. Think about this--it is perfect timing. When Christ was on the earth and His people, the children of Israel, rejected Him as a nation. At that time, He promised to graft the Jews who rejected Him back into His family. We must realize that the Jews will be an important part of the bride of Christ.

In Revelation 7, we see the turning-point. God is getting ready to move his saints out of harm's way through the Rapture, and He turns His attention to bringing the nation of Israel back into His family. He has just commissioned the 144,000 Jewish evangelists to preach Christ to the Jews throughout the world. Now you might wonder how God could pour out His wrath on the earth while His chosen people Israel are still on the earth. After further study, I believe once God seals the 144,000, there will be only a short time before the Rapture. During that short time, the 144,000 Jewish evangelists will launch the greatest evangelistic blitz of all time to let the Jews around the world know Jesus is their coming Messiah, and He is coming imminently to take them to His heavenly Father and introduce them as an important part of His bride.

I believe that when the Rapture occurs, many Jews will go up at this time. God will still extend His hand of protection to those who are left behind. I want to show you how I believe God will protect His people, the Jews who are left behind. The Bible teaches that the plagues cannot hurt the 144,000 sealed Jews. Read Revelation 9:1-6. *The fifth angel sounded his trumpet, and I saw a star that had fallen from the sky to the earth. The star was given the key to the shaft of the Abyss. When he opened the Abyss, smoke rose from it like the smoke from a gigantic furnace. The sun and sky were darkened by the smoke from the Abyss. And out of the smoke locusts came down upon the earth and were given power like that of scorpions of the earth. They were told not to harm the grass of the earth or any plant or tree, but only those people who did not have the seal of God on their foreheads. They were not given power to kill them, but only to torture them for five months. And the agony they suffered was like that of the sting of a scorpion when it strikes a man. During those days men will seek death, but will not find it; they will long to die, but death will elude them.*

When the Rapture occurs, those Jews who have just accepted Christ in this massive evangelistic effort will go up in the Rapture along with all the Christian Gentiles, including the dead in Christ and those Christians who are alive at that time. Recently, I believe God gave me further insight on a verse that previously confused me in Matthew 24:30-31. *At that time the sign of the Son of Man will appear in the sky, and the nations of the earth will mourn. They will see the Son of Man coming on the clouds of the sky, with power and great glory. And he will send his angels with a loud trumpet call and they will gather his elect from the four winds, from one end of the heavens to the other.*

I used to be confused as to why the nations of the earth would mourn at the time of the Rapture. Those who are left behind will have rejected Christ and accepted the antichrist as their god and they will not be mourning, they will be cursing the true and living God. I believe once someone takes the mark of the beast, they will no longer have a heart capable of repenting." So who is the nations of the earth refering to?

The King James Version uses the term "tribes" instead of "nations.". I believe this verse is speaking of the tribes of Israel in all the nations of the world. I believe when the 144,000 Jewish evangelists reach out to every Jew on earth, many will recognize Jesus as their Messiah and Savior and will go up in the Rapture. Those Jews who still reject this message will be allowed to witness Christ's coming in the clouds at the time of the Rapture. Those Jews will realize that they have just rejected Christ Jesus as their Messiah for the second time. The first time was at Christ's Crucifixion and then again at His Second Coming for His bride. The Jews from all nations around the world will mourn when they realize what they have done.

In the book of Zechariah, we read that at the time of the Second Coming and the battle of Armageddon, the Jews have their eyes opened, and they cry in repentance for rejecting Christ as their Messiah. Zechariah 12:10-11: *And I will pour out on the house of David and the inhabitants of Jerusalem a spirit of grace and supplication. They will look on me, the one they have pierced, and they will mourn for him as one mourns for an only child, and grieve bitterly for him as one grieves for a firstborn son. On that day the weeping in Jerusalem will be great, like the weeping of Hadad Rimmon in the plain of Megiddo.*

Now, let us return again to the subject of God's provision for His 144,000 special servants after the Rapture. The Bible says the Antichrist cannot harm them. When we carefully read Revelation 9:4, we understand it specifically points out that only God's 144,000, sealed with His mark, will be spared from this tormenting plague. This brings up two very important questions. The first is, "If there were tribulation saints, as many prophetic scholars believe, where is the provision for their protection from these plagues?" I consider this further reason to believe there are no tribulation saints after the Rapture. The second question is, "What will happen to God's chosen people Israel during this time?" I will show you how I believe God has made provision to protect His chosen people during this time.

Let us go back to the 144,000 Jews who have been sealed and commissioned to take the gospel of Christ to the nation of Israel. I believe part of their commission is to warn the Jews that Jesus is their Messiah, and He is coming for those who accepted Him. After this, the plagues of God's wrath will fall on the earth. I believe I can show you from God's Word that the children of Israel who miss the Rapture will be told to leave all nations where they are living and head back to the Holy Land before the plagues start to fall.

Remember when Moses told his people in Egypt to get ready for the Passover by sacrificing a lamb to cover and protect their homes and families from the angel of death? The 144,000 sealed Jews have this same kind of protection from the plagues that are about to come upon the earth. Remember when God was sending plagues like the locusts that ate all the crops of the Egyptians? If you read carefully about this account in the Old Testament, you will notice in the land of Goshen, the children of Israel were protected. The plagues did not harm the land of God's people. I believe it is possible to show from Scripture that God is going to call His people home to Israel just before His plagues and wrath fall upon man and the earth.

This is a good time to read Revelation 18, which talks about the fall of "Mystery Babylon." I have already said that I believe that "Mystery Babylon" is the United States, which happens to be the home of millions of Jews. Before the destruction of "Mystery Babylon," the Jews will be warned to leave. Remember, God's wrath and plagues start to fall in Revelation 8 **following** the Rapture. The saints in the United States and around the world have already left in the Rapture. The Jews who have not accepted Christ as their Messiah will be left behind at the time of the Rapture, but God will still make provision for them to escape His soon coming wrath.

Read Revelation 18:4. *And I heard another voice from heaven say, "Come out of her, my people, that ye be not partakers of her sins, and that ye receive not of her plagues."* I used to think that this was either a rapture verse or a command for Christians to leave the United States before God's wrath fell. There are two problems with this thinking. If this were a verse about the Rapture, God would not have to ask us to leave. We would just go instantly. If it were to mean the Christians are to leave the United States physically, then where would millions of Christians go? Would Canada or Mexico open its borders for all of these Christians? I do not think so.

Another writer on the End Times wrote an interesting explanation in his book on the last days. He said he believes the text in Revelation that says, *"Come out of her, my people,"* is speaking to American Christians, telling them to leave the United States and take flight to Israel for protection. I see a real problem with this interpretation. Do you believe that Israel will open its doors for millions of American Christians to come to Israel to wait for the Lord's return? I do not think so.

The only thing that makes sense to me is that God will instruct the Jews who missed the Rapture, after their indecision to accept Christ.

They will be warned by the 144,000 sealed Jewish evangelists to head for cover, to leave "Mystery Babylon" and the other nations of the earth, and to return to their homeland. Now think about this. If it were Gentile Christians trying to flee the United States, would Israel open its doors? Again, I do not think so. However, Israel has always had its doors open for the Jews to return to their own nation, Israel. I believe once these Jews flee to Israel, God will supernaturally protect them from harm just as he did the Jews in Egypt during the time of Moses.

A scripture verse that goes well with what I am sharing here is found in Ezekiel 39:27-28. *When I have brought them back from the nations and have gathered them from the countries of their enemies, I will show myself holy through them in the sight of many nations. Then they will know that I am the LORD, their God, for though I sent them into exile among the nations, I will gather them to their own land, not leaving any behind. I will no longer hide my face from them, for I will pour out my Spirit on the house of Israel, declares the Sovereign LORD.*

I covered more about the 144,000 in an earlier chapter where I showed how I believe these specially chosen Jews will be able to accomplish their mission for God with supernatural, resurrected bodies. The two witnesses will also have supernatural powers but will have mortal bodies, for the Bible clearly states that they will be killed and lay in the streets of Jerusalem for three and one-half days before being resurrected for the whole world to see (Revelation 11:7-13). These two witnesses will also be on the earth at the time when the Jews are being evacuated to Israel.

— CHAPTER SIX —

CAN GENTILES BE SAVED AFTER THE RAPTURE?

O ver the years, I have heard a few scenarios concerning this question. Some may ask, "But who are the Gentiles?" They are anyone from any nation or people group who are not Jewish.

1. One scenario could involve tribulation saints who knew about God's plan of salvation but did not accept Christ or live for Him before the Rapture. They would turn to Christ during the Great Tribulation and not accept the mark of the beast. They would struggle through the Great Tribulation and become the tribulation saints. This explanation is necessary in order to have a pre-tribulation rapture theory. If the Rapture does not happen until Revelation 7, then the term "tribulation saints" would not be necessary, for all the saints would be raptured at the same time. Further evidence of this scenario is the fact there is no mention of saints on the earth during the outpouring of God's wrath. Also, God makes provision for His wrath not to hurt the 144,000 Jews but makes no provision for tribulation saints! The best example is the scorpion creatures that cannot harm the 144,000 sealed with God's mark. Why is there no provision for the saints to be protected from these creatures of God's wrath? The best explanation is all the saints are raptured before this time of God's wrath on the earth.

2. Here is another scenario. The Holy Spirit would be removed during the Great Tribulation. The basis of this statement comes from the teaching that the saints are raptured off the earth and have the Holy Spirit living in them. When this happens, the Holy Spirit's influence will be taken off the earth with them. The question this generates in my mind is: if the Holy Spirit is not working to draw sinners to Christ, how will people be saved during this time? Some might say if you cannot accept and serve God with the Holy Spirit's help, how can you do it without the Holy Spirit's help? Yet as I see it, the Holy Spirit is God, who is omnipresent, and you cannot remove God from the earth.

3. My father-in-law, the Reverend Edgar Rasmussen, has always maintained that to tell people they can be saved after the Rapture is a shaky position at best. It gives people a false hope of a second chance. Holding out a second chance does not draw the unsaved and the backsliders to Christ. It tells them they can stay in their unsaved condition and still have a way back to God after the Rapture.

There are many who believe the saints have to be raptured before the Great Tribulation because the Bible says, *He that restraineth, must be taken out of the way before the antichrist can be revealed.* I believe this view has too many contradictions in God's Word. Basically, this view says the Rapture has to come before the antichrist can be revealed; therefore, the Rapture is a pre-tribulation event. But this interpretation contradicts 2 Thessalonians 2:3. *Don't let anyone deceive you in any way, for that day will not come until the rebellion occurs and the man of lawlessness is revealed, the man doomed to destruction.* I do not believe the restrainer is the Holy Spirit, and I will offer a compelling argument for who the restrainer is later in chapter nine .

My position on this question has become clearer while doing this study on the End Times. If we take the position that there is a pre-tribulation Rapture, then we have to assume the saints mentioned during the opening of the seals in Revelation 6 are tribulation saints. This is traditional thinking. As I have pointed out, if the Rapture does not happen until after the opening of the sixth seal in Revelation 6, actually happening in Revelation 7:9-13, then a very interesting observation can be made. Before I make this observation, I should point out that we can see the rapture event along with other important events happening in two sections of Revelation. We will see the 144,000 Jews and the Rapture following in both Revelation 7 and 14. You need to read these chapters together to get the whole picture, just as you would read the first four books of the New Testament to see the whole story of the Gospel.

This brings me to that very interesting observation I mentioned above and possibly the answer to the question, "Can Gentiles be saved after the Rapture?" If you look at Revelation 7 and 14, which contain the same rapture event, and if you continue reading on to the coming of Christ at the end of the Great Tribulation, you will see no living saints mentioned after the Rapture. Think about this: if the church has to go through the first half of the Great Tribulation, many exciting things will happen. Those who have fallen away will come back to Christ. The church will wake up and get the message of salvation out like never before in history, and as the day of the Gentiles is coming to a close after the sealing of the 144,000 Jews, every wise Christian will realize that we are in the final countdown of days on this side of eternity. Our 401k's will not do us any good, and only what is done for Christ will last. I believe that during this time, super-evangelism will be taking place, and all who will come to Christ will come. These will certainly be exciting times. Any tribulation we go through will be worth it in the end.

During this time, the church will see a time of spiritual warfare unlike anything the world has ever seen. Everyone will have to make a decision to either accept what Christ has to offer: eternal life with tribulation for a little while or the comfort and benefits of what the antichrist has to offer, a full belly. Hmmmm, is this not what Esau took for his birthright? The point is there will be no need for any more decisions to accept Christ after the Rapture. The time will be over for making decisions. I realize there will be exceptions to this; I believe there will be some people living in remote areas of the earth who will be outside of the influence of the antichrist, and if they survive the last years of the Great Tribulation, they will be included among those who will repopulate the earth during the millennium.

In closing, consider this. If the Rapture is pre-Tribulation, the church will continue in its lukewarm condition, waiting around for the Rapture while millions of people get left behind. On the other hand, with a mid-tribulation rapture happening after the opening of the seals during the first half of the Great Tribulation, then what happens in this instance is exciting. The church will wake up to what is about to take place, and we will see the greatest revival in the history of the church. I believe we will also see a great falling away at the same time. It is possible that when the church realizes what they were told about a pre-tribulation rapture was in error, many Christians will become bitter towards God. They may feel God has abandoned them, and they may give in to the New World system.

Even though this scenario is scary, look at the positive things that would happen. The church ushers in the greatest revival the world has ever seen, and the saints are purified into the pure bride for whom, the Bible says, Christ is coming back. This makes so much sense to me. Going through the trials of the first half of the Great Tribulation will purify and grow the bride of Christ. The Bible says in 2 Peter 3:9b, *He is patient with you, not wanting anyone to perish, but everyone to come to repentance.*

If I had my choice, the pre-tribulation rapture would be a far more desirable option. Even though the mid-tribulation scenario is a scary option, it means that millions more of the lost will come to Christ. Remember, many of those millions who have not accepted Christ are your friends and relatives! They are the ones for whom Christ died.

— CHAPTER SEVEN —

OTHER BIBLE TEACHERS' PERSPECTIVES CONCERNING THE RAPTURE

After studying the Bible and putting many of my thoughts on paper, I began an extensive search to look at other points of view about the Rapture. As this study progresses, I would ask that you have an open heart and mind. Remember, we are in search of the truth as revealed in God's Word.

The viewpoint of the pre-tribulation rapture is held by several denominational ministers and scholars. In order to search this out effectively, I will present scriptures and the thoughts that are used by teachers who support the pre-tribulation rapture.

The first teacher whose position I will examine has had a great ministry that teaches the chronology of God's dispensations and prophetic plans using a huge time line chart set up on the platforms of churches and auditoriums.

While this perspective is popular, I want you to consider that the pre-tribulation teachings may be flawed. Could it be possible that teachers of this position are defending a teaching to the point of possible spiritual blindness, a teaching handed down from their fathers and other generations before them?

I am not Paul, but what he wrote in the book of Acts is a worthwhile challenge to all of us, specifically in Acts 17:11. *Now the Bereans were of more noble character then the Thessalonians, for they received the message with great eagerness and examined the Scriptures every day to see if what Paul said was true.*

When I recently studied the small roll-out version of this chart, I noticed about a dozen Bible verses under the topic of the Rapture. Based on the placement of these verses on his chart, it is obvious that the chart represents a belief in a pre-tribulation rapture. The verses are placed on the chart between the seven churches of Revelation, found in Revelation 2 and 3, but before the opening of the seals, found in Revelation 6.

It is widely accepted that close to the opening of the seals is the beginning of the seven-year Great Tribulation period. Those who hold to the pre-tribulation view believe that the Rapture will take place before the Great Tribulation gets started. I studied through the list of verses on this teacher's chart, looking for ones that would show the timing of the Rapture. What I found in these verses was interesting. Basically, they attest to the resurrection of the righteous. They also attest to the Rapture, but they do not really show scripturally that the Rapture is a pre-tribulation event. In fact, there is one verse used that leans toward the Rapture being a post-tribulation event. Interestingly, this verse on the chart is the only one I have found so far that shows the timing of the Rapture as different from my conclusion about a mid-tribulation event. I will go over this verse in detail when I work my way through the verses on his list.

As I stated in a previous chapter, interpretation of scripture on any doctrinal issue should be backed up with at least two other verses in the Bible to assure the correct interpretation of God's Word. If I get confused over one verse because it contradicts my conclusion, I will stick with the interpretation I can back-up with two or more scriptures. I also believe that, as I continue to study God's Word, at some point the truth will come to light, and the verse that seems to contradict will eventually line-up with the rest of the Word of God.

Let us start by looking at the many Bible verses on the chart I mentioned above. I will show each verse, one at a time, and I will do my best to explain why it is relevant to the Rapture. I invite you to search with me to see if these verses actually show that the Rapture will be a pre-tribulation event.

SCRIPTURES UTILIZED TO TEACH A PRE-TRIBULATION RAPTURE

Luke 21:34-36, *Be careful, or your hearts will be weighed down with dissipation, drunkenness, and the anxieties of life, and that day will close on you unexpectedly like a trap. For it will come upon all those who live on the earth. Be always on the watch, and pray that you may be able to escape all that is about to happen, and that you may be able to stand before the Son of Man.*

When I read this over, I see it talks about a horrible time coming on the earth. I believe there are two periods to which it could be referring. The time of the Great Tribulation is the first that comes to mind, but the Bible teaches there will be a time of birth pains before the Great Tribulation starts that will be so bad that many will think the Great Tribulation has already started. I will cover this period of birth pains in more depth in the next chapter on the coming antichrist. These verses are a warning to Christians not to be so caught up in this world that we do not recognize the time in which we are living. We need to be sure that we are watching for the Lord's return so that we are not caught unawares. These verses infer that we can see this time coming, and it will not be a surprise to us. Luke 21:36, in particular, was probably used on this chart under the Rapture because it would be easy to assume that to escape what is to come means to escape the wrath of God. Luke 21:36, *Be always on the watch, and pray that you may be able to escape all that is about to happen.* The chart indicates by the scripture placement that we would escape by being raptured.

I want to remind you that if you are a Christian, you do not have to pray that you will go up in the Rapture. The Rapture will catch up every Christian and take us off this earth in the twinkling of an eye. I believe the Bible teaches us that Christians will go through some trying times and that our God is more than able to protect us in the midst of tribulation. As we see these times approaching, we need to pray that God will protect us and sustain us as we go through these times. His Word assures us we can count on His help. It is a given that we will escape God's wrath through the Rapture.

Look at Daniel's three friends who had to face the fiery furnace. God helped them escape that trial, and I believe if we make God our all-in-all by putting our total trust in Him, we will see Him miraculously preserve us in the worst of times. Yet, the Bible says there will be martyred saints during this time. Remember, we will never face any trial alone, for God's Word says, *"I will never leave you nor forsake you.* Also, when you look at the following verse in light of other scriptures, such as 2 Thessalonians 2:1-3, you see the Rapture may be getting close, but until certain events take place, it will not happen.

2 Thessalonians 2:1-3: *Concerning the coming of our Lord Jesus Christ and our being gathered to him, we ask you brothers, not to become easily unsettled or alarmed by some prophecy, report or letter supposed to have come from us, saying that the day of the Lord has already come. Don't let anyone deceive you in any way, for that day will not come, until the rebellion occurs and the man of lawlessness is revealed, the man doomed to destruction.*

I know the man doomed to destruction is the antichrist and he is yet to be revealed. For the longest time, I did not know what the rebellion was about, but now I realize it is a great falling away that will take place before the Lord returns. This verse is talking about the coming antichrist and the falling away in the same verse. I believe that is because the falling away will happen during the time of the antichrist. After continued study I now realize that the falling away will start before the antichrist arrives. It is sad, but the church today is weak, and I believe many Christians are convinced the Rapture will take us to heaven before times get tough. If the church suddenly sees the hard times of the Great Tribulation and is not prepared for it, when faced with the choice of whether to buy into the antichrist's system or be denied the ability to buy or sell and face possible starvation, many will make the wrong choice. I believe this will be the time of a great falling away. In chapter nine I will expand on this great falling away when I cover my time line chart to the Rapture. As I have warned previously, Esau sold his birthright for food, so according to God's Word, the time will not be right for the church to be gathered to Jesus in the Rapture until we see these two events come to pass. In chapter ten, I cover a total of six events that must take place before the Rapture can occur.

The next verse presented in the pre-tribulation chart is John 14:1-3. *Do not let your hearts be troubled. Trust in God; trust also in me. In my Father's house are many rooms, if it were not so, I would have told you. I am going to prepare a place for you. I will come back and take you to be with me, that you also may be where I am.*

This is a great verse full of the promises of God. It has much to say to the church, but I will share three points that are relevant to my study:

This verse attests to the resurrection of God's people.

It says Christ is coming back to receive His elect or saints to Himself.

It attests to the fact there will be a rapture, but there is no indication of the timing of the Rapture in relation to the Great Tribulation.

The next verse is I Corinthians 15:23. *But each in his own turn: Christ, the first fruits; then, when he comes, those who belong to him.*

This verse is quite self-explanatory. Jesus is coming for His bride. There is a rapture on the horizon. It says when He comes, those who belong to him will be resurrected. The ones who belong to Him are the Christians and the Jews who have accepted Christ. The Bible says we will each go in his own time. Yet there is still no indication of the Rapture event's timing in this verse.

The next text is 1 Corinthians 15:51-58. *Listen, I tell you a mystery: We will not all sleep, but we will all be changed -- in a flash, in the twinkling of an eye, at the last trumpet, for the trumpet will sound, the dead will be raised imperishable, and we will be changed. For the perishable must clothe itself with the imperishable and the mortal with immortality. When the perishable has been clothed with the imperishable, and the mortal with immortality, then the saying that is written will come true: "Death has been swallowed up in victory." Where, O death is your victory? Where, O death is your sting? The sting of death is sin, and the power of sin is the law. But thanks be to God! he gives us victory through our Lord Jesus Christ. Therefore, my dear brothers, stand firm. Let nothing move you. Always give yourselves fully to the work of the Lord, because you know that your labor in the Lord is not in vain.*

This is a great portion of scripture; it not only talks about the Rapture but also goes into great detail on how we will be changed into eternal beings. In light of God's grace, it behooves us to give all of our life and strength to the work of the Lord in whatever capacity God calls us.

This next verse has confused me a bit about the timing of the Rapture. Remember, this popular end-times chart promotes the pre-tribulation rapture. I am leaning heavily toward a mid-tribulation rapture, even though I would prefer a pre-tribulation rapture. (I think we all would prefer the easy way!) This verse gives evidence of a post-tribulation rapture. Read 1 Corinthians 15:52. *...in a flash, in the twinkling of an eye, at the last trumpet, for the trumpet will sound, the dead will be raised imperishable, and we will be changed.*

The phrase, *...at the last trumpet...*, begs the question, which last trumpet? The only last trumpet I am aware of is the last trumpet of the seven trumpets of God's wrath. I do not believe we will go through the wrath of God under the category of the seven trumpets. I believe, with study, this inconsistency will be reconciled, for there are too many scriptures placing the Rapture in Revelation 7 **before** the wrath of God. I would rather stay with an interpretation with multiple verses to support it. Later, in chapter eleven, I will explain an alternative to the last trumpet, and the accompanying inconsistency will go away.

After four years of working on this study, I now lean toward a mid-tribulation rapture because of the amount of scriptural support to back up this position. We especially need to weigh the scriptures that are plain and easy to understand as we attempt to build a doctrinal position. If the scriptures we use are vague, we could be building our position like building a house of cards.

The next verse in the end times chart is 2 Corinthians 5:1-8. *Now we know that if the earthly tent we live in is destroyed, we have a building from God, an eternal house in heaven, not built by human hands. Meanwhile, we groan, longing to be clothed with our heavenly dwelling, because when we are clothed, we will not be found naked. For while we are in this tent, we groan and are burdened, because we do not wish to be unclothed but to be clothed with our heavenly dwelling, so that what is mortal may be swallowed up by life. Now it is God who has made us for this very purpose and has given us the Spirit as a deposit, guaranteeing what is to come. Therefore, we are always confident and know that as long as we are home in the body we are away from the Lord. We live by faith, not by sight. We are confident; I say and would prefer to be away from the body and at home with the Lord.*

These verses attest to the resurrection and the promise of a new eternal body. They give us an expectant hope in the future of exchanging our earthly body for an eternal one that will allow us to live with Christ forever. However, these verses give no indication about the timing of Christ's return or the placement of the Rapture even though they give us significant assurance God has better things for us ahead for all eternity.

The verse shown next on the pre-tribulation rapture chart is Ephesians

5:27, which states, *...and to present her to himself as a radiant church, without stain or wrinkle or any other blemish, but holy and blameless...* Again, this verse attests to the resurrection of the believer, but there is no mention of the Rapture or the timing of Christ's coming.

Next, read Philippians 3:11 *...and so, somehow, to attain to the resurrection from the dead...* and 3:20-21, *But our citizenship is in heaven. And we eagerly await a Savior from there, the Lord Jesus Christ, who by the power that enables him to bring everything under his control, will transform our lowly bodies so that they will be like his glorious body.*

These verses also speak about the resurrection and our mortal bodies being transformed to be like Christ's glorious body. I can see these verses touching on Christ's power to bring about the Rapture, but there is no indication about the timing of this event.

Next, read Colossians 3:4. *When Christ, who is your life, appears, then you also will appear with him in glory.* This verse surely refers to the Rapture. It clearly says when Christ appears, we will be in glory with Him, but it gives no indication of timing for the Rapture.

The following verses for study are from the book of 1 Thessalonians:

1 Thessalonians 2:19: *For what is our hope, our joy, or the crown in which we will glory in the presence of our Lord Jesus when he comes? Is it not you?* This verse attests to the resurrection and Christ's coming for us, but again there is no indication of timing.

1 Thessalonians 3:13: *May he strengthen your hearts so you will be blameless and holy in the presence of our God and Father when our Lord Jesus comes with all his holy ones.* This verse points to Christ's coming for His saints, but as with the other verses, it gives no timing for the Rapture.

1 Thessalonians 4:13-17: *Brothers, we do not want you to be ignorant about those who fall asleep, or to grieve like the rest of men, who have no hope. We believe that Jesus died and rose again and so we believe that God*

will bring with Jesus those who have fallen asleep in him. According to the Lord's own word, we tell you that we who are still alive at the coming of the Lord, will certainly not precede those who have fallen asleep. For the Lord himself will come down from heaven, with a loud command, with the voice of the archangel and with the trumpet call of God, and the dead in Christ will rise first. After that, we who are still alive and are left will be caught up with them in the clouds to meet the Lord in the air. And so we will be with the Lord forever. This is a tremendous passage of scripture that affirms the resurrection of both the dead in Christ and those who are alive at His coming. It is saying, when Christ comes, those who are alive will be taken by the Rapture and not by death.

The next verse to examine is 2 Thessalonians 5:9-23. I will not write out this whole section of scripture, but all of chapter five should be read in this study. This chapter begins by discussing times and dates and being caught unprepared for Christ's coming.

I will, however, quote the first six verses of 1 Thessalonians 5:1-6. *Now, brothers, about times and dates we do not need to write to you, for you know very well that the day of the Lord will come like a thief in the night. While people are saying "Peace and safety," destruction will come on them suddenly, as labor pains on a pregnant woman, and they will not escape. But you, brothers, are not in darkness so that this day should surprise you like a thief. You are all sons of the light and sons of the day. We do not belong to the night or to the darkness. So then, let us not be like others who are asleep, but let us be alert and self-controlled.*

The church should not be caught by surprise at the coming of the Lord; it is only the unsaved world around us who are crying, "Peace and safety," who will be surprised as if by a thief in the night. Looking at 2 Thessalonians 5 as a whole is so important in understanding the Lord's coming, yet there is no sign of the timing of the Rapture.

The next verse posted on the pre-tribulation rapture chart is 2 Thessalonians 2:1. *Concerning the coming of our Lord Jesus Christ and our being gathered to him...* This verse attests to Christ's coming and the

Rapture, but like the other verses it fails to provide any indication of timing. It is important to note that if this chart would have included the next two verses after 2 Thessalonians 2:1, we would see that Paul is telling the church that the Rapture will not happen until certain events take place. The key event is the revealing of antichrist. Therefore, this verse in full context gives some support to a mid-tribulation rapture.

Next, 2 Thessalonians 2:7, 8: *For the secret power of lawlessness is already at work; but the one who now holds it back will continue to do so till he is taken out of the way. And then the lawless one will be revealed, whom the Lord Jesus will overthrow with the breath of his mouth and destroy by the splendor of his coming.* These last two verses are quite interesting. They are generally accepted as referring to the antichrist, and many believe that these verses are about the collective power of spirit-filled Christians being able to restrain the antichrist. Therefore, the Rapture is looked at as the way that the restrainer would be taken out of the way, giving the antichrist free reign on the earth. If you really think about this explanation and look closely at these scriptures, you will see a problem with this explanation. Look at the portion which says, but the one who now holds it back will *continue* to do so till he is taken out of the way. This verse describes the restrainer as "the one," not a collective force, such as from masses of Christians. I have always had a problem believing that Christians have to be raptured before the antichrist could have free reign. If the collective force and power of all praying saints could restrain the antichrist, then why did not the prayers and collective power of all Christians restrain Hitler and other tyrants who have lived and attacked Christians and Jews on the earth, including stopping all the Christians from being martyred throughout the ages?

Most Christians who believe in a pre-tribulation rapture also believe there will be tribulation saints after the Rapture. Some denominations believe that the tribulation saints will be comprised of those who had drifted away from God before the time of the Rapture but came back to God after missing that event. There are some churches that believe a few, who may have thought they were Christians by their good works or simply by being a part of a church, will be left behind, much to their surprise. As I have come to my conclusion that the Rapture will be a mid-tribulation event, I do not see that scriptures support the idea of tribulation saints after the Rapture. All who will come back to God or get saved during the early years of the Great Tribulation will have made up their minds to serve God or not, and when the Rapture occurs, those who are not Christians will have fully rejected Christ. The reason I bring up this idea is because those who believe there will be tribulation saints would have to infer that tribulation saints would be helpless without the power of the Holy Spirit. Think about this. Could it be that scriptures are actually referring to someone else being taken out of the way? I will go into detail to answer this question in chapter nine where I talk about the four strongest arguments for the pre-tribulation rapture.

I do not mean to come off like a know-it-all, but I believe I have a reasonable explanation for who "he" is that has to be taken out of the way, in order to give the antichrist full reign on the earth. Do you remember the story of when Daniel fasted and prayed for God's intervention? He was visited by the Lord and His top warring angel, Michael the Archangel.

Read Daniel 10. Here are a few good verses to consider: First, Daniel 10:12, 13 (KJV): *Then said he unto me, fear not, Daniel: for from the first day that thou didst set thine heart to understand and to chasten thyself before thy God, thy words were heard, and I am come for thy words. But the prince of the kingdom of Persia withstood me one and twenty days: but, lo, Michael, one of the chief princes, came to help me; and I remained there with the kings of Persia.*

Next read Daniel 10:20, 21 (KJV): *Then said he, Knowest thou wherefore I am come unto thee? And now will I return to fight with the prince of Persia: and when I am gone forth, lo, the prince of Grecia shall come. But I will shew thee that which is noted in the Scriptures of truth: and there is none that holdeth with me in these things, but Michael your prince.*

So my explanation for this verse is that one of God's most powerful angels, Michael, is the one who is holding the antichrist at bay until it is time for Satan to unleash his full fury of evil on the earth, and he, Michael, will have to be taken out of the way or be told to halt his restraining work, not the church. I would have to say that the only verse that shows the timing of the Rapture as pre-Tribulation is this one here. Yet, if you agree that the church through the ages has not really been a restraining force with the power to stop evil, then you may conclude as I have that this scripture does not provide scriptural proof that the Rapture will happen before the antichrist is revealed or before the Great Tribulation starts. I will be going into greater detail on Michael the Archangel in a later chapter, showing why I believe that he is the restrainer who must be removed or told to stand down.

I will now examine a second teacher who also supports the pre-tribulation position. I will be drawing my discussion from a popular book on the subject of the Rapture and the End Times. The first statement in that book which caught my attention is that the scriptures clearly support a pre-tribulation rapture of believers. Please understand my motives in examining the teachings of these scholars. I have come to a point where I just do not think the pre-tribulation viewpoint of the Rapture is clearly supported by scripture. Yet, I hear this teacher make the statement that the Bible clearly supports the pre-tribulation viewpoint.

I see the mid-tribulation view of the Rapture clearly supported in the Bible. Some people might ask, "Just what difference does it really make?" If it did not make any difference, I would not be writing this, but it will make a huge difference when the Great Tribulation starts and millions of believers realize the Rapture did not happen. They will be upset at their Bible teachers and pastors who misled them. Please do not take offense at this last statement. I would love for a Bible teacher or pastor to show me clear scriptural support for a pre-tribulation rapture, but because our views on the timing of the Rapture are so opposed, I have to examine their evidence to see which view really is clearly supported by the Word of God.

The book I am drawing this discussion from covers five reasons for believing that the Rapture is a pre-tribulation event. I will examine each of the author's five scriptural reasons for his position in this context. I will then look at the author's views as compared to my position, which has evolved into a mid-tribulation Rapture position. You can decide for yourself which position is clearly supported by the Word of God.

The first reason for supporting a pre-tribulation position uses the following scripture reference. Revelation 19:11, 14 (KJV): *And I saw heaven opened, and behold a white horse; and he that sat upon him was called Faithful and True, and in righteousness he doth judge and make war.* Also, *The armies which were in heaven followed him upon white horses, clothed in fine linen, white and clean.* If we look at the context of the text, we will notice it is the nineteenth chapter of Revelation. The wrath of God is finished and Christ is returning with His saints. I agree with the author's statement that the saints have to go to heaven before this event happens in order for the saints to come back to the earth with Jesus from heaven. This teacher does not address the fact that if the Rapture is a mid-tribulation event, as shown in the second half of Revelation 7 before the wrath of God starts in Revelation 8,the saints would be in heaven in more than enough time to return with Christ as indicated in Revelation 19.

The author of this book makes the comment that the post–tribulation position is not logical. I agree with the author on this point because the post–tribulation position teaches that the Rapture does not happen until the end of God's wrath. The main point I would like to make is that his first scriptural support for a pre-tribulation rapture does not contradict the mid-tribulation position. Therefore, the Word of God is not clearly supporting a pre-tribulation rapture from this scripture verse.

The second argument for a pre-tribulation rapture from the author's book on the Rapture and the End Times is from Revelation 7. The author points out how the four angels who have power to harm the earth are told to hold back until the 144,000 Jews are sealed. He then goes on to say that if there is no sealing of Christians to protect them, then they must be already raptured; therefore, on that basis, he sees the Rapture as a pre-tribulation event. If you read Revelation 7, where the 144,000 are sealed, the Rapture from the mid-tribulation view occurs sometime after the sealing of the 144,000 in Revelation 7, but before the wrath of God is poured out in Revelation 8.

What is interesting is that the author states that the sealing of the 144,000 is before God's wrath. God never pours His wrath upon the righteous. Look closely and you will see that at the point of the sealing of the 144,000, the six seals of Revelation 6 have already been opened. In this case, the author says that the seals are not the wrath of God. At other times, he says the seals are the wrath of God. I will give further reasoning why the seals are not part of the wrath of God in chapter nine . The mid-tribulation view I share in this study goes on to say the saints, or the church, will go through the opening of the seals of Revelation 6. Then the 144,000 Jews will be sealed in Revelation 7, and after the sealing of the 144,000, the mid-tribulation Rapture will take place before the wrath of God begins in Revelation 8. Again, the author's second argument for a pre-tribulation Rapture does not conflict with the mid-tribulation view. Therefore, this scripture passage does not clearly support the pre-tribulation view of the Rapture.

This teacher's third argument for a pre-tribulation Rapture is that the restrainer must be taken out of the way. He uses 2 Thessalonians 2:6-8 *And now you know what is holding him back, so that he may be revealed at the proper time. For the secret power of lawlessness is already at work; but the one who now holds it back will continue to do so till he is taken out of the way. And then the lawless one will be revealed, whom the Lord Jesus will overthrow with the breath of his mouth and destroy by the splendor of his coming.* When we read this scripture carefully, we see the antichrist cannot be revealed until the restrainer is taken out of the way. So if the restrainer is the church or the saints on earth, then the antichrist cannot be revealed until after the Rapture of the church. When we read 2 Thessalonians 2:1-3, we really have a problem: *Concerning the coming of our Lord Jesus Christ and our being gathered to him, we ask you brothers not to become easily unsettled or alarmed by some prophecy, report or letter supposed to have come from us, saying that the day of the Lord has already come. Don't let anyone deceive you in any way, for that day will not come until the rebellion occurs and the man of lawlessness is revealed, the man doomed to destruction.* This scripture says that before the church can be gathered to Christ, the antichrist must first be revealed. His argument totally contradicts 2 Thessalonians 2:6-8. That text says that the restrainer must be removed first. Which is it? You cannot have it both ways. If the restrainer is not the church, the problem goes away. I cover this contradiction later in this study, pointing out it makes more sense that the restrainer is not the church but is Michael the Archangel, the chief warring angel who came to Daniel's aid when he prayed and fasted for twenty-one days. But the bottom line is that this third argument from the book on *The Rapture and the End Times* is not clearly supporting a pre-tribulation rapture.

The last two points in the book, supporting this author's view, are handled as one, so I will try to cover them as one. First, the author says, "The Lord commands the church to always be watchful for Christ's coming." Then he goes on to say, "...which could happen at any time...", quoting 1 Thessalonians 5:6 and Luke 12:40. *Therefore let us not sleep, as do others, but let us watch and be sober.* Then it says, *Be ye therefore ready also: for the Son of Man cometh at an hour when ye think not.* As I look at 1 Thessalonians 5:6 where it says "...but let us watch...", my question is this: If the Lord's coming and the Rapture are without warning, why do we have to watch? If we are told to watch, there has to be something for which to watch. Furthermore, if there is something for which we are to watch, then how can we say that the Rapture is an imminent event? For an event to be imminent, by definition, there cannot be anything that has to happen before that imminent event. If there is anything that has to happen, for which we have to watch and wait, then that event is not imminent.

The author's viewpoint is interesting because he teaches that the Rapture has been an imminent event for two thousand years. My question is, "If we had to wait for Israel to be reborn as a nation, which happened in 1948, then how could the Rapture have been imminent before 1948?" Also, the apostle Paul talks about the Lord's coming and our gathering to Him as not taking place until the man of lawlessness is revealed. Read 2 Thessalonians 2:1-3. *Concerning the coming of the Lord Jesus Christ and our being gathered to him, we ask you, brothers, not to become easily unsettled or alarmed by some prophecy, report or letter supposed to have come from us, saying that the day of the Lord has come. Don't let anyone deceive you in any way, for that day will not come until the rebellion occurs and the man of lawlessness is revealed, the man doomed to destruction.* So how can anyone say the Rapture is imminent if the man of lawlessness is not revealed? Does it not make sense that the Rapture will not be imminent until sometime after the antichrist is revealed? There are other events that must also take place before the Rapture. I will discuss these events in chapter ten.

Some people say no man knows the day or the hour of the Lord's return. I agree with this, as this is what the Bible says, and once the antichrist is revealed, we will still not know the day or the hour of Christ's return. It will be time for us to obey the words in Luke 21:25-28. *There will be signs in the sun, moon and stars, on the earth; nations will be in anguish and perplexity at the roaring of the sea. Men will faint from terror, apprehensive of what is coming on the world, for heavenly bodies will be shaken. At that time, they will see the Son of Man coming in a cloud with power and great glory. When these things begin to take place, stand up and lift up your heads, because your redemption is drawing near.* If we have to wait for these things to begin to come to pass, and if we have been commanded to watch for these things, then how can we say the Rapture is imminent?

In closing, the book on *The Rapture and the End Times* quotes from <u>Webster's Ninth New Collegiate Dictionary</u>, which defines "imminent" as ready to take place, especially hanging threateningly over one's head. The author explains that a fellow colleague noted in his book on the End Times, "Other things may happen before the imminent event, but nothing else MUST take place before it happens...If something else must take place before an event can happen, that event cannot be counted as imminent."

The author concludes that because the Rapture is pre-tribulation, it has to be imminent. But this statement is based on flawed, scriptural support. If the Rapture is a mid-tribulation event, then it cannot be imminent until the Great Tribulation is in motion, the 144,000 are sealed, the antichrist arrives, and other events take place. In closing, the author's last scriptural arguments do not clearly support a pre-tribulation rapture.

The third teacher I will be critiquing has written many books and taught many times on television, often covering topics concerning the Rapture and the End Times. The other night when I was watching television, I noticed he was teaching on the Rapture, and he said that there are some people teaching that the church is going through the Great Tribulation. He said, "Let me shoot that down right here." When he said that, I was all ears. At the time I started this study, I had a multitude of questions on the timing of the Rapture. I had always held to the pre-tribulation view of the Rapture. It was my hope when I started this study, I would find scriptural strength from the Word of God to prove to myself that the pre-tribulation view is the correct view. However, as this study progressed, the opposite has happened. I am now convinced that the mid-tribulation view of the Rapture is the most accurate interpretation, based on the weight of scripture from God's Word. When this teacher said, "Let me shoot the mid-tribulation rapture teaching down right here," he had my attention.

Thank God for a DVR on my television. I record my favorite

evangelists every day so that I can listen to them on my schedule. I replayed this teachers program several times, about why the Rapture is a pre-tribulation event. I dug out several Bibles to check his Bible quotations, and this is what I found.

The teacher began by explaining that the first three chapters of Revelation talk about the seven churches of Asia, and after that, the church is not mentioned again until the end of the book of Revelation. "Why?" he asked. "Because the church goes up in the air."

He went on to say that in Revelation 4:1, John was snatched up into heaven where he saw the twenty-four elders who were seated, robed, and crowned. The teacher used the phrase "snatched up into heaven." But this is not what the Bible states. This phrase makes it sound as if this is a Rapture event while, in reality, the verse simply says, "...Come up here." When it is time for the Rapture, God will not be asking us to come up because, without notice in the twinkling of an eye, we will be "...caught up..." We will not be asked to come up.

The television evangelist continued his teaching, saying because the elders are wearing robes and crowns; this represents the church. I see a problem with this interpretation. First, I do not read of a multitude that would represent the saints or the church in heaven in white robes until Revelation 7:9. *After this I looked, and there before me was a great multitude that no one could count, from every tribe, people, and language standing before the throne and in front of the Lamb. They were wearing white robes and were holding palm branches in their hands.* If you read this carefully in the book of Revelation, you will notice it does not mention this multitude as having crowns. Why? A good explanation for this is the saints will not be given crowns until the Judgment Seat of Christ for believers takes place. It is reasonable to believe this judgment of believers will not happen until all of the saints are in heaven. Doesn't it make sense that the saints being martyred in Revelation 6 at the fifth seal would not receive their crowns and rewards until all the saints are united in heaven? The first pre-tribulation teacher who used the time line chart puts this judgment of believers during the period when God is pouring out His wrath on the earth (after the Rapture of all believers). Then the Marriage Supper of the Lamb happens after the Judgment Seat of Christ. This makes sense to me.

If the saints and the church have to wait to receive their rewards until all the saints are in heaven, then how can someone say the elders in Revelation 4:4 represent the church wearing their robes and crowns? Therefore, the reference to the elders wearing robes and crowns in Revelation 4:4 must point to the twenty-four elders. They would be in heaven before the Rapture and could have already received their crowns that represent the rewards for what they did with their lives on earth. I have read that many people believe the twenty-four elders are leaders from the twelve tribes of Israel and the twelve disciples. This makes sense to me, but other people say they would not be in heaven around the throne until the Rapture of the church. I can see two scriptural reasons why they can be in heaven before the Rapture of the church.

The first reason is found in Matthew 27:51-52, These verses are about what happened when Christ died on the cross and was later resurrected. The Bible says, *At that moment, the curtain of the temple was torn in two from top to bottom. The earth shook and the rocks split. The tombs broke open and the bodies of many holy people who had died were raised to life.* These holy people were resurrected after Christ was resurrected, and they were seen by many people. Also, if God chose to take Enoch and Elijah to heaven before they died, and if God resurrected these holy people at the time of Christ's resurrection, then it is not a violation of scripture to imagine God could resurrect the twenty-four elders before the church is resurrected at the Rapture.

The second reason is found in Revelation 7:13-14. *Then one of the elders asked me, 'These in white robes -- who are they, and where did they come from?" I answered, "Sir, you know." And he said, "These are they who have come out of the Great Tribulation..."* Revelation 7:9 says a great multitude in white robes suddenly appeared in heaven. I see this plainly describing the Rapture. So how can the elders represent the church in Revelation 4:4 if the multitude in white robes does not appear in heaven until Revelation 7:9? They do not represent the church; they are just the twenty-four elders who are at the throne of God when the church arrives in Revelation 7.

The television preacher explained that the church is raptured in Revelation 4, and the antichrist shows up in Revelation 6. He went on to say that if four comes before six, then we are out of here. If you want to stay, that's your business. But consider the wording of 2 Thessalonians 2:1-4. *Concerning the coming of our Lord Jesus Christ and our being gathered to him, we ask you, brothers, not to become easily unsettled or alarmed by some prophecy, report or letter supposed to have come from us, saying that the day of the Lord has already come. Do not let anyone deceive you in any way, for that day will not come until the rebellion occurs and the man of lawlessness is revealed, the man doomed to destruction. He opposes and exalts himself over everything that is called God or is worshiped, and even sets himself up in God's temple, proclaiming himself to be God.*

Here we see clear wording. Paul is teaching that the Rapture, or as Paul says, "...the gathering to him....", will not take place until the antichrist is revealed. If the antichrist is not revealed until Revelation 6, then the Rapture cannot happen until sometime after the revealing of the antichrist occurs in Revelation 6. I hope it is clear that, based on the Word of God. With all due respect, I cannot agree with this television preacher.

— CHAPTER EIGHT —

THE COMING ANTICHRIST

W hen I first wrote the outline for this study, I included a chapter on the antichrist. Well, as this study was taking shape, it seemed that all I would be writing concerning the antichrist would be a rehash of what everyone else had said or written. I felt unless I had something fresh to write, I should just drop this topic from my study. A few weeks later, as I was reading the book of Revelation, two fresh truths jumped out at me. As I studied further to confirm if I was seeing the Word of God correctly, I had further insights jumping out at me. At that point, I realized I had to write this chapter.

To begin with, I must set the backdrop where I believe the antichrist first appears on the world's stage. If you will read the following verses, I will explain where I am going with this. Read Revelation 13:1-3. *And I saw a beast coming out of the sea. He had ten horns and seven heads, with ten crowns on his horns, and on each head a blasphemous name. The beast I saw resembled a leopard, but had feet like those of a bear and a mouth like that of a lion. The dragon gave the beast his power and his throne and great authority. One of the heads of the beast seemed to have had a fatal wound, but the fatal wound had been healed. The whole world was astonished and followed the beast.*

I do not pretend to understand all that is written in these verses, but what I do understand, I will explain. These verses begin with a beast coming out of the sea with ten horns, ten crowns, and seven heads, and it is a bit confusing, but what we can infer is the beast is a rising government which will grow to become one-world government. The passage describes one of the heads of the beast as seeming to have a fatal wound. From this verse, I conclude that the antichrist will come from one of the heads of the beast. What is interesting is before one of the heads of the beast is wounded, the whole being described here as the beast with ten horns (or ten leaders or heads of state) must be fully in place. Once the antichrist comes from one of the heads of the beast, <u>then</u> the antichrist is referred to as "the beast." If you read the following verses, it will help clarify the description of the beast that becomes a one-world government consisting of ten kings or leaders. Read Revelation 17:12 and 14. *The ten horns you saw are ten kings who have not yet received a kingdom, but who for one hour will receive authority as kings along with the beast. They will make war against the Lamb, but the Lamb will overcome them because he is Lord of lords and King of kings and with him will be his called, chosen and faithful followers.*

As a point of clarification there have been many world leaders who have had the spirit of antichrist, but just having the spirit of antichrist does not make them the antichrist. Hitler certainly had the spirit of antichrist, but he was not *the* antichrist. If you believe as I do that the man who will become the antichrist is alive on the earth today, you have to realize even though he is destined to become the antichrist, he will not be the antichrist until Satan literally possesses his body and brings him back from death.

Now, if we draw from the accepted teaching about the coming antichrist, we will see most prophetic teachers believe that the man who will become the antichrist will be the leader of this one-world government, and then this world leader will be mortally wounded. Many believe he will have a mortal head wound, and his miraculous recovery will usher in the antichrist. Let's read Revelation 13:3. *One of the heads of the beast seemed to have had a fatal wound, but the fatal wound had been healed.* **This verse does not say the leader of this one-world government will be wounded. NO!! It says one of the <u>heads</u> of this government will be wounded. This means to qualify as a candidate for the antichrist, you must be one of the ten heads.** Let me further explain. The European Union is getting ready to elect a permanent leader to lead the countries or regions that are aligned with this new one-world government. Tony Blair, the former leader of England, is one of the leaders who has tossed his hat into the ring to run for this position. I have already heard of Bible teachers who believe that Tony Blair is going to be the antichrist. But no, this is not what is being said in the Bible. **The Bible says one of the ten heads is fatally wounded, not the leader of the ten heads.**

An important point to understand is the event that leads to one of the ten heads of state being fatally wounded cannot occur until the one-world government is in place. This means that according to 2 Thessalonians 2:1-3, the gathering of believers or the Rapture cannot occur until the one-world government is in place and the antichrist is revealed.

Many Bible teachers are now saying the future one-world government will not be comprised of ten nations but ten <u>regions</u> of the world. The ten crowns and ten horns represent ten leadership positions. This verse says one of the heads is wounded with a fatal wound, which means the leader over the ten heads or the president of the European Union does not qualify to become the antichrist. He must be one of the heads of the beast to qualify. Now, if you think about this, any one of these ten horns or heads of state that comprise the new one-world government could end up being the antichrist. This means that we will not know for certain who the antichrist is until one of the ten heads of state is fatally wounded.

The powers behind the formation of this future one-world government have already laid out the division of this future global government. The future antichrist must come from one of the following regions. It is from this global division that we get the ten heads of the beast.

1. America, Canada and Mexico

2. South America

3. Australia and New Zealand

4. Western Europe

5. Eastern Europe

6. South Asia

7. Central Asia

8. North Africa

9. South Africa

10. The Middle East

If we refine this list a bit further, we realize that some of these ten regions don't qualify to produce the antichrist. We know the Russian region and the Asian region both have separate parts to play in end-times prophecy, and the leaders from these regions would not be the antichrist. We know that the Middle East region will accept a seven-year peace pact with the antichrist, and Israel would never go along if the antichrist came from the Middle East region. This brings the list of ten down to seven. If you look further at the leaders of the other regions, some of them are a lesser caliber then what would probably be accepted by the world as the new global leader, thus making it easier to see who of these leaders will rise as the antichrist.

This leads to another interesting thought. If any one of the heads that comprise the one-world government can be tapped to become the antichrist, then consider the following idea. I only know of one End Times teacher, Dr. Jack Van Impe, who has said our current president is being groomed to be "The Man." I have said all along I just do not see how he could be "The Man," but personally, I do not know of

Wow!

wow

any leader who is more qualified. If you are following my reasoning here, you may come to the same conclusion as I. If the United States becomes the North American region of the new world government, and its leader is the president, then the president would become one of the heads of the beast. This would make the President of the United States a qualifying person who could become the antichrist. WOW! What a thought.

Another important thought to keep in mind as these events start to unfold is this: BEFORE the United States would be willing to sign up and join the one-world government and become part of the North American region of this global government, the United States has to fall apart economically, as well as suffering a complete breakdown of society as we know it. A period of time from between six months on the short side and up a year and a half on the long side could occur before we would be willing to give up our independence. We might see events like terrorist attacks on our cities, hyper-inflation, and the collapse of our dollar, food shortages, famine, and anarchy in our cities. This stretch of time will seem like the end-of-the-world to many. Many Christians will believe the Great Tribulation has started. This period of time is only part of the birth pains that will be coming on the world before the Great Tribulation begins, merely setting the stage for the antichrist to come to power. Personally, I believe this period, before the Great Tribulation starts, will be on the short side of my predictions. Once things start falling together, world events will move rapidly to the prophetic destiny of the Lord's return.

Imagine how these coming events will affect our lives. This coming time of upheaval will be a window that will last from the time the world economies collapse until the ten-region, one-world government is formed. This window will be unlike any time in American history. Life as we know it will be over. This special window will last until the antichrist comes to power. We need to be ready to take advantage of the greatest evangelistic opportunity the world has ever seen. People's lives will be turned upside down.

Churches will be filled with people looking for answers. If we know this time is coming, we can prepare to have a part in this great harvest of souls. Once the antichrist comes to power, this open window to share Christ's love will close.

Recently, as I was preparing this study for the printers, I was watching a well-known televangelist. He was talking about the soon-coming collapse of the dollar and America's economic collapse. He made the statement that he knows when this is going to happen. He then predicted that America's dollar and economy would collapse when the church is raptured out of here. This statement is giving a false sense of security to all his followers. If you recognize from this study that the one-world government has to be in place before the Great Tribulation starts, then you must also realize that the church will see a period of tribulation, even if the Rapture were a pre-tribulation event. I would not want to be in the shoes of this preacher when the US economy collapses, and his church fills up with all these people who are asking him, "Where is the Rapture that is supposed to get us out of here?" The store shelves will have been emptied by panic-buying. People will not be ready for what lies ahead. In fact, I believe most of the churches in America are not ready for what lies ahead.

If you have followed me this far, you will realize this one-world government will have a leader who does not become the antichrist. This global government will probably be faltering, and the stage will be set for a greater leader to rise from its ranks. Then, when one of the heads of the beast or one of the leaders of this ten-region, one-world government is fatally wounded and lies at death's door, he will be brought back to the land of the living. He will arise with the wisdom and the cunning of Satan. He will show the world he is the one they are to follow. Read Revelation 13:3. *One of the heads of the beast seemed to have had a fatal wound, but the fatal wound had been healed. The whole world was astonished and followed the beast.*

Another verse that helps to understand the nature and makeup of the beast is found in Daniel 7:20-21. *I also wanted to know about the ten horns on its head and about the other horn that came up, before which three of them fell - the horn that looked more imposing than the others and that had eyes and a mouth that spoke boastfully. As I watched, this horn was waging war against the saints and defeating them.* The portion of this verse that says *The horn that looked more imposing than the others* is a phrase that gives evidence that one of the ten horns will rise up from the others to become the antichrist. Once this horn or head of state has been fatally wounded, he will come back as Satan in the flesh, and then it will be evident who the antichrist is.

Wow!

Another verse that gives many insights to the nature of the antichrist is found in Daniel 8:23-25. *In the latter part of their reign, when rebels have become completely wicked, a stern faced king, a master of intrigue will arise. He will become very strong, but not by his own power. He will cause astounding devastation and will succeed in whatever he does. He will destroy the mighty men and the holy people. He will cause deceit to prosper and he will consider himself superior. When they feel secure, he will destroy many and take his stand against the Prince of princes. Yet he will be destroyed but not by human hands.*

These verses give some incredible insights to this coming global leader. First, the scripture says he will be a master of intrigue. When you look up the word "intrigue" in the dictionary, what you learn is this leader is a master of deceit and lies. This global leader will make war against all that is good and against God's people. He will even stand up against the Prince of princes, yet he will be defeated but not by human hands. Can it be any clearer? Jesus will win, and we win. Come, Lord Jesus.

As we study the scriptures, we will come to realize there is one sure way to know who the antichrist is before his coming to power. The Bible says he who has wisdom may be able to figure it out. Revelation 13:18 (KJV) says, *Here is wisdom. Let him that hath understanding count the number of the beast: for it is the number of a man; and his number is Six hundred threescore and six.* Think about this. If the antichrist were to be the leader of the European Union, such as Tony Blair, it does not take any wisdom at all to figure out who the antichrist would be – the president of the European Union. However, if you try to figure out which of these ten horns or leaders is to be the antichrist, you would need to see all of these leaders' birth certificates so that you could see the name with which they were born. The original birth certificate of one prominent world leader, who could some day be one of the ten leaders of this new world government, is cloaked in uncertainty and not available for close examination. *He is refering to obama* *no one has seen birth certificate*

As we continue to study Daniel 7, we will see more hints as to what kind of leader the antichrist will be. These hints could help discern who of the ten world leaders will be the antichrist. The first hint is found in Daniel 7:20b, *...the horn that looked more imposing then the others and that had eyes and a mouth that spoke boastfully.* This verse says this leader will be imposing in stature, boastful and arrogant. Unfortunately, many world leaders match this description. Then read Daniel 7:25a. *He will speak against the Most High and oppress his saints and try to change the set times and the laws.* This leader will be a leader who will bring in many changes to customs and established laws.

An important point to consider is a one-world government must be in place <u>before</u> one of the ten heads of state can be fatally wounded, and this has to happen before the antichrist can rise to power. This seriously puts the imminent return of the Lord on hold until a one-world government is in place.

Next, I want to point out that we have been misled concerning the kind of mortal wound this world leader would have. As I mentioned earlier, most Christians believe the world leader would recover from a fatal head wound. This is taken from Revelation 13:3a. *One of the heads of the beast seemed to have had a fatal wound, but the fatal wound had been healed.* **This verse does not say this leader will recover from a head wound. No, what it is saying is one of the ten heads of the beast is fatally wounded. What does "one of the heads" mean? What**

Read + understand !

it means is the beast is comprised of a number of leaders or heads of state, and one of these ten heads of state is fatally wounded but not necessarily from a wound to the head. Why is this important? I believe this event will reveal the antichrist and the beginning of the Great Tribulation will soon follow. If most Christians have been taught the antichrist would arise after a miraculous recovery from a fatal head wound, then when this leader does not recover from a head wound but maybe from a fatal wound to other vital organs, this will leave many confused. They will not know if this really is the antichrist. When the antichrist rises to deceive even the elect, if possible, he will have confused Christians who are open to deception.

Another point, that could lead to confusion concerning who the antichrist is, could originate with the type of wound that this world leader receives. I have heard teaching that this leader who is fatally wounded will be wounded from a sword. The Bible does say he is wounded with a sword. Revelation 13:14b (KJV): *...saying to them that dwell on the earth, that they should make an image to the beast, which had the wound by a sword and did live.* The point I would like to make is, when John the Revelator wrote this, the weapons we have today did not exist. When my wife and I traveled across the country doing Kids Crusades, we did a message on the whole armor of God. We substituted modern weapons for the weapons used by a Roman soldier in Bible days. For the Sword of the Spirit, we substituted a rifle. It is possible the future antichrist will be wounded with a sword, but I do not believe we should be adamant about what type of weapon will be used. John the Revelator had never seen a rifle.

CHAPTER NINE

PRE-VS.-MID-TRIBULATION VIEW OF THE RAPTURE

For most of my thirty-eight years as a Christian, I have held to the pre-tribulation view of the Rapture and know this position quite well.

A challenge I would like to make to the readers of these next two chapters is to, first, have an open mind. Then, either prove my conclusions to be wrong with sound arguments from the Word of God, or shout my conclusions from the housetops. There can be no middle ground. To be wrong on this doctrine would leave the church ill-prepared for what we will face leading up to the Lord's return.

I want to look at the four strongest arguments for the pre-tribulation Rapture position and then look at the soundness of each of these teachings in light of the mid-tribulation position.

1. The restrainer must be removed.

I am going to start off with one of the most common scriptural verses that scholars who believe in the pre-tribulation rapture use to support this viewpoint. It is found in 2 Thessalonians 2:7-8a. *For the secret power of lawlessness is already at work; but the one who now holds it back will continue to do so till he is taken out of the way. And then the lawless one will be revealed.*

The pre-tribulation position states that the restrainer is the Holy Spirit or the Spirit-filled church that holds back the coming reign of the anti-christ. The reason this verse is so important to the pre-tribulation position is because those holding this position believe that as long as the church is on the earth with the indwelling Holy Spirit, the Holy Spirit's power in us will restrain the antichrist from fully rising to power. **I have mentioned earlier in this study that I see a weakness in this interpretation. I do not see either scriptural or actual evidence that the Spirit-filled believers have been able to restrain evil on the earth. We could not restrain Hitler or the evil of other tyrannical leaders of the past. When the saints were being tortured in Rome, Spirit-filled Christians could not stop the martyrdom of the saints, so why do we think we have the power to hold back the antichrist now?**

I would like to propose a question to help solve a second problem regarding the belief that God needs to remove the Holy Spirit (and thus the church) in order to keep us from preventing the antichrist's rise to power. "Does God answer all our prayers affirmatively?" No! God answers our prayers if they are in His will. If we pray for something outside of the will of God, He will not grant our petition. When you think about the greatest attacks in history against those whom God loved, you realize those attacks always led to great victories. Without the enslavement of the Israelites in Egypt, we would not have seen the exodus. Without the persecution of eighty thousand Christians by Chairman Mao in China, there would not be one to two hundred million Christians in China today. Without Hitler and the Holocaust, Israel would not have been reborn as a nation. Without the crucifixion of Christ, we would not have our salvation. Without the coming of the antichrist, we would not have the coming of the Lord. The question I would like to pose is, "Would it have been possible, through prayer, to have stopped these events from happening?" We know from God's Word that Jesus had to go to the cross; this event could not be stopped. I do not believe these other events were supposed to be stopped. I believe during extraordinary times of persecution, the church and believers are to pray for personal intervention and protection. During these times, believers need to pray for the salvation of people our lives touch. We need to look at these times of tribulation as opportunities to win the lost and accomplish God's will.

Before it is time for the Lord to come back, will it be God's will for the antichrist to come to power? The answer is "yes!" So, if it is God's will for the antichrist to come to power, why would God answer our prayers to prevent the antichrist from coming to power? Therefore, if God is not going to answer prayers that are contrary to His will concerning the antichrist, then why would God have to remove the church for this reason? Yet if removing the church is the correct interpretation of this verse, where is the weight of other scriptures to back it? To the best of my knowledge, they are totally absent.

The next question is, "If we have been misinterpreting this scripture, what would be an alternative interpretation, and does that view have the strong weight of scripture to back it?" I will now give a scripturally-backed alternative as to why I believe the first position I have discussed is wrong. The alternative position that keeps getting stronger as I study this is that the restrainer referred to here is Michael, God's chief warring angel. Jude 9 refers to Michael as the archangel. Webster's dictionary says an archangel is an angel of high rank.

After Daniel had fasted and prayed for twenty-one days, he had an encounter with the Lord, and an angel told him it took all of those days to break through spiritual battles. Daniel 10:13 describes this experience. *But the prince of the Persian kingdom resisted me twenty-one days. Then Michael, one of the chief princes, came to help me, because I was detained there with the king of Persia.*

This verse is saying Michael is one of God's top warring angels who can step in to help us when we call out to God for help. Plus, Michael has the power to restrain evil. To me, this is compelling, but is there weight from other scriptures to back up this idea? Read Daniel 12:1. *At that time, Michael, the great prince who protects your people, will arise. There will be a time of distress such as has not happened from the beginning of nations until then.*

This is a very compelling verse. First, it talks about Michael, the Great Prince who protects God's people. From whom is Michael protecting God's people? Spiritual forces of wickedness, undoubtedly. Then notice the context here is during the time of the end. **Now, if Michael, one of God's generals who commands the armies of God, can protect us from evil forces, then does it not make sense that if God wants to allow the forces of evil to rise up on the earth in the person of the antichrist, that God could tell Michael, one of his top Generals, to stand-down?**

During World War II, we had a few top generals who commanded the U.S. armed forces. One was General MacArthur in the Pacific theater of the war, and another was General Patton commanding the Third Army in Europe. When the war against the Germans and the Japanese was coming to a close, both of these generals wanted to press onward. General MacArthur wanted to roll into China and prevent it from being a future problem, and General Patton wanted to continue to roll into Russia and stop the threat of communism under Stalin. Well, when push came to shove, they had a Commander-in-Chief they had to obey. The President of the United States, Harry Truman told both of these generals to stand-down. So does it not make sense that God can tell His leading general, Michael, "the restrainer of evil," to stand-down?

There is another story to illustrate this point. I saw a Disney movie one time in which a bear cub was out on its own, and a great lion was stalking the little bear. When the bear cub saw the lion, he became bold and rose up to stand against this great beast. All of a sudden, you could see the look of fear on the lion and it ran away. Then they showed the huge mother bear standing tall behind the little bear cub. It was not the cub, after all, that made the lion flee. It was the mother that was backing the cub up that put fear into the lion. It is almost like the church thinks we are the ones who can hold the antichrist back, but no, it is the armies of God under Michael the Archangel's command who are holding back the powers of evil.

Again, do we have the weight of scripture to support this argument? There are so many stories in the Bible about angels executing God's judgment and being instruments of delivering God's children when they sought Him for help. The first verse I will show is found in the story of Sodom and Gomorrah, Genesis 19:12-13. *The two men said to Lot, "Do you have anyone else here, sons in law, sons or daughters, or anyone else in the city that belong to you? Get them out of here, because we are going to destroy this place. The outcry to the Lord against its people is so great he has sent us to destroy it."* These men were angels.

In another example, God sent an angel of judgment against Jerusalem and later told this angel to stand-down. Read 1 Chronicles 21:15. *And God sent an angel to destroy Jerusalem, but as the angel was doing so, the Lord saw it and was grieved because of the calamity and said to the angel who was destroying the people, "Enough! Withdraw your hand."* Another example is in 2 Chronicles when Hezekiah put his trust in the Lord to fight his battles. When God answered Hezekiah's prayer, the Lord sent angels to fight the forces of evil. The passage in 2 Chronicles 32:7-8 says, *Be strong and courageous. Do not be afraid or discouraged because of the king of Assyria and the vast army with him, for there is a greater power with us than with him. With him is only the arm of the flesh, but with us is the Lord our God to help us and to fight our battles.*

This next verse shows how God answered their prayers for help. In 2 Chronicles 32:20-21, the Word says, *King Hezekiah and the prophet, Isaiah, son of Amoz, cried out in prayer to heaven about this. And the Lord sent an angel who annihilated all the fighting men and the leaders and officers in the camp of the Assyrian king.* In 2 Kings, there are a few examples that show what kind of aid is available when we seek God's help and intervention. The first is found in 2 Kings 6:15-17. *When the servant of the man of God got up and went out early the next morning, an army with horses and chariots had surrounded the city. "Oh my Lord, what shall we do?" the servant asked. "Don't be afraid," the prophet answered. "Those who are with us are more than those who are with them." And Elisha prayed, "O Lord open his eyes so he may see." Then the Lord opened his eyes and he looked and saw the hills full of horses and chariots of fire all around Elisha.*

Next, read what happens to their enemies when God fights the battles for them in 2 Kings 19:35. *That night the angel of the Lord went out and put to death a hundred and eighty-five thousand men in the Assyrian camp. When the people got up the next morning, there were all dead bodies!* Also, let us not forget about the apostles who were thrown into prison for their witness for Jesus. When they were thrown into prison, angels came to their rescue as spoken of in Acts 5:18-19. *They arrested the apostles and put them in the public jail. But during the night an angel of the Lord opened the doors of the jail and brought them out.*

God's Word even says in the last days, at the time of the Lord's return, God will send angels to protect us from anyone who tries to harm us. What a promise in God's Word! It says in 2 Thessalonians 1:6-7, *God is just: he will pay back trouble to those who trouble you and give relief to you who are troubled, and to us as well. This will happen when the Lord Jesus is revealed from heaven in blazing fire with his powerful angels.*

There is much weight in the Word of God to prove that angels are the powers God uses to restrain. It is not the church that is the restrainer who is keeping the antichrist from coming to power, but it is the armies of God commanded by God's general, Michael the Archangel. The day is soon coming when the Commander-in-Chief will issue the order for the armies of God to stand-down. When that day comes, Michael may not want to go along with it, but he will stand down, and all hell will break loose on the earth.

I have to wonder if the following Bible verses that I have pondered for a long time could have something to do with what I have been describing here. Read Revelation 12:12b. *But woe to the earth and the sea, because the devil has gone down to you! He is filled with fury, because he knows that his time is short.* It gets even more convincing when you go back a few verses and read Revelation 12:7-9. *And there was war in heaven. Michael and his angels fought against the dragon, and the dragon and his angels fought back. But they were not strong enough, and they lost their place in heaven. The great dragon was hurled down, that ancient serpent, called the devil or satan, who leads the whole world astray. He was hurled to the earth, and his angels with him.* Now if you will skip a few verses ahead to Revelation 13:3, you will see what happens once chaos begins to break loose on the earth, for then the antichrist will truly be recognized after surviving a fatal wound. Revelation 13:3: *One of the heads of the beast seemed to have had a fatal wound, but the fatal wound had been healed. The whole world will be astonished and follow the beast.*

Review what I have been saying and showing you from the Word of God. It is not the church or the Holy Spirit; rather, it is Michael the Archangel, who is the restrainer of evil. If you will ponder these last verses I have just discussed in Revelation 12 and 13, it makes so much sense to me the restrainer of evil has just waged a great battle in the heavens, and Satan and his followers have just lost their place in heaven. The Bible says that Satan has had a place in heaven where he would go to God and bring accusations against the brethren or against God's people. Now he has just lost his place in heaven. Read Revelation 12:10, *Then I heard a loud voice in heaven say, "Now have come the salvation and the power and the kingdom of our God and the authority of his Christ. For the accuser of our brothers, who accuses them before our God day and night has been hurled down."*

Is there any doubt who has just restrained the power of wickedness here? It was Michael and the armies of God who have just cast Satan to the earth. I can imagine a bit here. Michael has just kicked Satan out of the heavens, and he has just won the war God commanded him to fight. Now if you will think about how General Patton and General MacArthur wanted to press on and finish off the enemies of the earth for all time, this is how I imagine Michael would similarly go to the

Commander-in-Chief to seek permission to press on with the battle. I can hear Michael making his appeal to our heavenly Father, "This is our chance. Satan and his minions have been pushed back. We have them right where we want them. Just say the word, and I will command your armies to take satan out for all time." Then God replies, "No, Michael, your assignment is completed. I have a different plan for satan. It is now time for you and the armies you command to stand-down." Michael realizes God, in His infinite wisdom, has everything under control. This is where we need to read 2 Thessalonians 2:7-8a. *For the secret power of lawlessness is already at work, but the one who now holds it back will continue to do so till he is taken out of the way. And then the lawless one will be revealed.* If you will read this verse carefully, you will see it says the antichrist will not be revealed until the restrainer is taken out of the way.

When you think about this and about what we just covered in the book of Revelation, chapters 12 and 13, it is just a few verses after Satan is thrown down to the earth that a world leader is fatally wounded and then comes back from the dead as the antichrist! It makes sense to me that once Satan is thrown down to the earth, this will be the point when the restrainer has been removed.

You may have to be like the Bereans and read and study the Bible verses I have outlined, but what I have presented in this study is very compelling.

2. God has not appointed us to wrath.

There are two good verses in the Bible that support the teaching that God has not appointed us to suffer the wrath of God that will take place during the Great Tribulation.

The first is found in 1 Thessalonians 5:9. *For God did not appoint us to suffer wrath but to receive salvation through our Lord, Jesus Christ.*

The second is found in 1 Thessalonians 1:10. *And to wait for his Son from heaven, whom he raised from the dead - Jesus, Who rescues us from the coming wrath.*

From the pre-tribulation rapture viewpoint, these verses indicate the Rapture is a pre-tribulation event to spare the church from the coming wrath during the Great Tribulation.

Consider that the Bible calls the time period leading up to His return, "the Great Tribulation", a seven-year time period that will become more and more intense as Christ's coming approaches. The Bible likens the increase of severe events to birth pains. I believe we are currently entering the time of the birth pains predicted. They could become so severe some Christians may believe the Great Tribulation has started, but if you look at the beginning of the Great Tribulation, with the opening of the seven seals, you will see events that are similar to what has happened for all of time: wars, earthquakes, famine, even the martyrdom of the saints, to which the fifth seal refers. Just as when a woman is getting closer to delivering a child and the intensity of her labor pain increases, that is how it will be when the seals are opened at the beginning of the Great Tribulation.

The intensity of war will increase, earthquakes will be more devastating, and famines will be widespread. Most Christians who hold to the pre-tribulation rapture believe we will miss out on the seals and all of the Great Tribulation.

Many quote 1 Thessalonians 1:10 to try to prove that point. If you look closely at this verse, it says, ...*Jesus who rescues us from the coming wrath.* This means the wrath of God. This verse does not say we will be delivered from tribulation to come. In fact, **think about it; the Great Tribulation is not called the Great Wrath of God**. To me, it is obvious the seals are not the wrath of God, for God does not start wars, bring famine (and certainly he does not martyr His saints) as described in the fifth seal.

I believe the wrath of God does not start until Revelation 8 and 9, and then it picks up again in chapter fifteen. On the other hand, let us consider what the Bible teaches about tribulation. The Bible says that tribulation "worketh patience." It is interesting during the Great

Tribulation, when the saints are battling with the antichrist. God's Word says in Revelation 13:10, *...if anyone is to go into captivity, into captivity he will go, if anyone is to be killed with the sword, he will be killed. This calls for patient endurance on the part of the saints.* I believe the Bible is teaching that the saints will be going through a period of tribulation that will bring about the purification of the body of Christ.

Does not the Bible teach us that Christ is coming back for a pure bride, worthy of being called the bride of Christ? To put this into further biblical context, read Revelation 13:7-10: *He was given power to make war against the saints and to conquer them. And he was given authority over every tribe, people, language, and nation. All inhabitants of the earth will worship the beast - all whose names have not been written in the book of life belonging to the Lamb that was slain from the creation of the world. He who has an ear, let him hear. If anyone is to go into captivity, into captivity he will go. If anyone is to be killed with the sword, with the sword he will be killed. This calls for patient endurance and faithfulness on the part of the saints.*

These verses are describing several different scenarios believers will be subjected to during the first part of the Great Tribulation. Basically, this is calling for our unswerving faithfulness and testimony to Christ. Some Christians will be thrown into jail and others will be killed, but we just have to stay true to Christ, knowing they can take our lives but not our eternal souls!

One question I have to ask is, "Does God's Word further support this teaching that the saints will go through a period of tribulation and persecution during this time at the end called the Great Tribulation?" I believe the Bible does give further weight to this thought in 2 Thessalonians 1:4-6: *Therefore among God's churches we boast about your perseverance and faith in all the persecutions and trials you are enduring. All this is evidence that God's judgment is right, and as a result you will be counted worthy of the kingdom of God, for which you are suffering. God is just; he will pay back trouble to those who trouble you.*

As you read further in this chapter, specifically verses 7-10a, you will notice the context for this chapter very much concerns the coming of the Lord. These verses are talking about a future time when Christ is revealed and returns to punish those who do not obey the gospel. The passage in 2 Thessalonians 1:7-10 says, *And give relief to you who are troubled and to us as well. This will happen when the Lord Jesus is revealed from heaven in blazing fire with his powerful angels. He will punish those who do not know God and do not obey the gospel of our Lord Jesus. They will be punished with everlasting destruction and shut out from the presence of the Lord and from the majesty of his power on the day he comes to be glorified in his holy people and to be marveled at among all those who have believed. This includes you, because, you believed our testimony to you.*

These verses are talking about a time of tribulation the saints will have to endure. These verses are also addressing the church. They clearly say the timeframe for this tribulation and the persecution of the saints will be during the time of the end, leading up to the Lord's return.

Earlier in my study, I mentioned I did not know what the rebellion was. Look at 2 Thessalonians 2:3 in the Kings James Version. You will notice the rebellion is referred to as a great falling away of believers. This is a key point for my position of a mid-tribulation rapture. I hear so many people say, "What difference will it make whether the rapture is pre-trib. or mid-trib. anyway? It will all pan out in the end."

I feel there is a huge difference. What would have happened if Noah had not built the ark or if Joseph had not prepared for the famine in Egypt? How will millions of Christians feel who have been taught Christ is coming to Rapture His church away before the Great Tribulation starts, when suddenly, the world is thrown into chaos? Imagine if Al Qaeda successfully pulls off their plan, which they have had in the works for many years, called the Hiroshima project. The project calls for Al Qaeda terrorists to set off seven or more nukes in seven or more major cities in the United States on the same day. World trade would come to a halt. All the food from store shelves would disappear in panic buying. Most major cities would be overrun with anarchy. All of a sudden, we would be thrown into great tribulation. This event could lead to the global collaspe of world economies,ultimately forcing the nations of the world to join a newly formed one world govenment.

From the collapse of the world economies to the forming of the one-world government could be six to eighteen months. This collapse will bring nations to their knees and make them willing to give up their independence and sovereignty as an individual nation to join the one-world government. Unfortunately, it is highly possible that those six to eighteen months will be a time of anarchy and famine and destitution on earth, but that does not mean the Great Tribulation has begun. The Great Tribulation cannot begin until the one-world government is in place. The Bible references ten heads of government forming the new one world government will be in place. Remember, the trigger event for the beginning of the tribulation is the seven-year peace pact with Israel, which cannot happen until the antichrist creates that peace pact.

My concern, and one of the greatest reasons why I am writing this book, is that millions of Christians at that time will question the teachings of their churches and wonder why the Rapture has not occurred. There is the potential for hundreds of thousands of Christians to feel that they were betrayed by their teachers and abandoned by God. When you consider this, you can see how the stage would be set for a great falling away that is talked about in the Bible.

And what about suffering? Some Christians today question that God would actually allow us to suffer through the Great Tribulation and emphatically believe that God would never abandon us to the torment of the antichrist. I do not want to be a pessimist or create fear, but it is important to know that while most Christians in the West have enjoyed great religious liberty, there have been more Christians martyred for their faith in the last century than in the previous centuries combined since the time of Christ. That is a documented fact. Persecution and martyrdom have stepped up significantly in the 20th and 21st centuries.

In fact, if we were alive as adults during Hitler's era, most of us have surmised that Hitler was the antichrist and that the Tribul had begun with the annihilation of millions of Jews.

Suffering is not new to the Jew or the Christian. Have you ever rea *Foxe's Book of Martyrs?* This book covers centuries of Christians who were killed for their unswerving faith in Christ, from the deaths of Christ's disciples and the persecution by the Roman Church in 1200 A.D. to the persecution and killing of Christians a few centries ago that caused them to leave their mother country and come to America for freedom of religion. I am not talking about water-boarding, which some in our society label as torture. NO! I am talking about Christ's disciple Peter being crucified upside down because he did not feel worthy to die the same death as Christ his Lord. I am talking about Christians being beheaded, torn apart by wild beasts, boiled to death, and burned at the stake.

One story that has always stuck in my memory is the story of a Christian who was to be burned at the stake, and he told a friend nearby that he believed God's grace would be sufficient for him to bear up to this death. The friend told the sentenced man that if God's grace is sufficient, raise one finger to let him know. When the flames were engulfing him, he raised up two fingers signifying God's grace was more than enough. When I hear pastors and Christians say God would never abandon His church, I am reminded of Christ's death on the cross when Christ cried out in Matthew 27:46 (KJV): *And about the ninth hour Jesus cried with a loud voice, saying "Eli, Eli, Lama Sabachthani." That is to say, My God, my God, why hast thou forsaken me?* Did God forsake Jesus Christ His Son? Only in the sense He allowed His Son to die for our sins. If we as Christians have to suffer and die for our faith as martyrs did in ages past, does this mean God has forsaken us? No, because I am reminded of God's promise in Hebrews 13:5b-6: *...because God has said, "Never will I leave you; never will I forsake you." So we say with confidence, "The Lord is my helper, I will not be afraid. What can man do to me?*

st part of the Great Tribulation will be a time of great
tion that will wake up many in today's Laodicean-type
all believers to become the pure bride, without spot or
m Christ is coming back. Most importantly, I believe
have a major part in the harvest of the lost souls who
or the Rapture. To back up this thought, look at the
Revelation has to say about the Laodicean church, namely
n 3:19-21: *Those whom I love I rebuke and discipline. So be
t, and repent. Here I am! I stand at the door and knock. If anyone
rs my voice and opens the door, I will come in and eat with him and
he with me. To him who overcomes, I will give the right to sit with me on
my throne, just as I overcame and sat down with my Father on his throne.*
What a thought! Could Jesus be knocking on the door of our churches,
calling the backslidden to come back to Him with all their hearts? Also
notice that God is giving rewards to those who overcome. In order to
be an overcomer, there must be trials and tribulation to overcome.

In conclusion, I agree with the pre-tribulation view that God has not
accounted us to the wrath to come. However, I part company with the
belief that the seals are the wrath of God. Up until now, I have believed
the seals **are not part** of the wrath of God because the fifth seal is the
martyrdom of the saints. God would not do this to His own.

Some time ago, I was talking to a pastor friend of mine about the
timing of the Rapture. When I told him my viewpoint on the wrath of
God, he said he believed the four horses or the first four seals are the
wrath of God. Well, the first thing that entered my mind was the first
horseman who is the revealing of antichrist. Therefore, how could this
be the wrath of God? Then the thought hit me regarding the second
seal; that shows peace would be taken from the earth. Again, this just
does not sound like the wrath of God. Looking at the fourth seal, it
says in Revelation 6:7-8: *When the Lamb opened the fourth seal, I heard
the voice of the fourth living creature say, "Come!" I looked and there before
me was a pale horse, its rider was named Death, and Hades was following
close behind him.* This sounds more like the devil, and it sounds like it

is coming out of hell and not from God.

I did not express all of these thoughts to my pre-tribulation, believing pastor friend. However, as I was driving home, I had a conversation out loud with God, and I kept asking how I might show or explain that the wrath of God does not happen until Revelation 8 with the seven trumpets of God's wrath. I kept asking what is the difference between the seals and the wrath of God. It was like this thought just popped into my head. (I believe the Holy Spirit answered my question right there on the spot). **The thought that came to me was, "The difference is in the delivery." Angels deliver all of the seven trumpets of God's wrath; angels also deliver the last seven bowls of God's wrath, BUT angels are nowhere involved with the opening of the seals in Revelation 6.** When I arrived home and studied my Bible, all these thoughts were confirmed from God's Word.

A couple of interesting points that go along with this conclusion are about the scroll. Revelation 5:2-3: says, *I saw a mighty angel proclaiming in a loud voice, "Who is worthy to break the seals and open the scroll?" But no one in heaven or on the earth or under the earth could open the scroll or even look inside it.* **What I notice here is the seals are not <u>in</u> the scroll, they are on the <u>outside</u> of the scroll, and the wrath of God is inside the scroll!** *correct*

Also, when we look at the many examples of God's judgment on the nations, we continually see angels involved in the delivery of judgment. There is the angel of death in Egypt and the angels again in Sodom and Gomorrah. Also, there is the angel of the Lord who slew 185,000 Assyrians in one night and the angel who killed thousands in Jerusalem when David took the census against God's wishes. I have to say the weight of scripture is compelling here; angels are involved in God's wrath and there are no angels involved with the seals.

I further believe the Rapture is clearly described in Revelation 7, before the wrath of God begins in Revelation 8 and 9. What I will do in the next section of this chapter is show why I believe Revelation 4:1 does not describe the Rapture. I will also explain why I believe Revelation 7:9 <u>IS</u> describing the Rapture. I think I can show that scripture leans heavily on the Rapture occurring in the seventh chapter of Revelation.

In closing, I believe we will have to go through some unprecedented times. Yet, I am prepared in my heart, knowing in whom I have believed and am persuaded that He is able to protect me against that day. Man may hurt my mortal body, but man cannot hurt my eternal soul.

3. Revelation 4:1: The open door to heaven

Revelation 4:1: says, *After this I looked, and there before me was a door standing open in heaven. And the voice I had first heard speaking to me like a trumpet said, "Come up here, and I will show you what must take place after this."* Then Revelation 4:2: says, *At once I was in the Spirit, and there before me was a throne in heaven with someone sitting on it.*

These verses from Revelation 4:1-2 are interpreted to symbolically represent the Rapture of the church. I just do not see the Rapture of the church in these verses. I see John, the Revelator, being taken to heaven to the very throne of God where God told him, "I will show you what must take place after this." If you will go to Revelation 19:11, you will see heaven opened up again just like what happened in Revelation 4:1. Read Revelation 19:11: *I saw heaven standing open, and there before me was a white horse, whose rider is called Faithful and True. With justice he judges and makes war.* This is a revelation of Christ after the battles have been won and the marriage supper of the Lamb is about to take place. This door standing open does not mean a gateway is open for a rapture event because if you will go back to Revelation 19:6-8, you will discover the saints are already in heaven about to celebrate with Christ at the marriage supper of the Lamb. Read Revelation 19:6-8: *Then I heard what sounded like a great multitude, like the roar of rushing waters, and like loud peals of thunder, shouting: "Hallelujah, for our Lord God Almighty reigns. Let us rejoice and be glad and give him glory, for the wedding of the Lamb has come, and his bride has made herself ready. Fine linen, bright and clean, was given her to wear."*

I would like to know where to find a second or third scripture that shows the timing of the Rapture before the Great Tribulation starts. I was taught in Bible school that doctrine has to be backed with the witness of two or three other scriptures.

Now I will point out a third scripture verse that shows Paul, in this case, being caught up to heaven to see special revelations from God, just like John the Revelator. What Paul experienced does not represent a symbolic rapture of the church either. Read 2 Corinthian 12:3-4: *And I know that this man - whether in the body or apart from the body I do not know, but God knows - was caught up to Paradise. He heard inexpressible things, things that man is not permitted to tell.* Paul's experience is very similar to that which John the Revelator experienced. In fact, in Paul's case, he was "caught up" to Paradise, while John was asked to "Come up here." When the Rapture occurs, we will not be asked to come up; we will be caught up.

What I see happening here by those who want to interpret Revelation 4:1 as the Rapture of the church is they are strengthening their position on this doctrine based on the symbolic meaning of what they see in this passage. I believe all doctrine must be supported by the "plain speak" Word of God, and then let symbolism confirm it. We should not rely on symbolism alone. When you look at Revelation 4:1, it does not say the church is caught up to heaven. In fact, it does not even use the words, "caught up." No. Bible scholars have determined there is a symbolic meaning here, and our traditions have accepted it.

I firmly believe we should never interpret scripture symbolically to establish a doctrinal position. A doctrinal teaching must first be established as literal from the Bible. Symbolic use of scripture should only be used to supplement and support what the Bible teaches elsewhere literally, or you can make the Bible say anything you want. This type of interpretation is how cults are established.

I want to show you there are Bible verses that <u>plainly</u> speak of the Rapture. I will show you these verses, and then I will show you why Revelation 4:1 does not qualify as a verse that can be used to symbolically support the timing of the Rapture. This is very important to understand because, for someone who holds to the pre-tribulation view of the Rapture, Revelation 4:1 is really the only verse that alludes to the Rapture happening before the Great Tribulation begins. This means the timing of the Rapture as a pre-tribulation event is being established by the use of the symbolic meaning of Revelation 4:1, and that makes for shaky interpretation.

The first verse I will use to show the Rapture is 1 Thessalonians 4:16-17: *For the Lord himself will come down from heaven, with a loud command, with the voice of the archangel and the trumpet call of God, and the dead in Christ will rise first. After that we who are alive and are left will be caught up with them in the clouds to meet the Lord in the air. And so we will be with the Lord forever.*

Notice we who are alive are caught up in the clouds to meet the Lord in the air. Next, I will show you other verses that support the Lord's coming in the clouds to meet us at the time of the Rapture. Read Matthew 24:30-31: *At that time, the sign of the Son of Man will appear in the sky and all nations of the earth will mourn. They will see the Son of Man coming on the clouds of the sky, with power and great glory. And he will send his angels with a loud trumpet call, and they will gather his elect from the four winds, from one end of the heavens to the other.* Without writing them out, if you look up these other scripture verses, you will again see the Lord is meeting us in the clouds in Luke 21: 26-27 and Mark 13: 26-27.

Now as you study these verses, it is easy to see that the Lord will come in the clouds, and we are caught up in the clouds to meet the Lord in the air. When you go back and look at Revelation 4:1, John was not caught up in the clouds. In fact, he was not caught up at all. He was told to "Come up here."

Another point, John was not caught up at all. Revelation 4:1 says, *After this I looked, and there before me was a door standing open in heaven. And the voice I had first heard speaking to me like a trumpet said, "**Come up here**, and I will show you what must take place after this."*

When the Rapture happens, we are not asked to come up; we are <u>caught up</u>! God does not have to ask or tell us to come; we will be caught up instantly, in the twinkling of an eye. This verse is sometimes interpreted to mean the church is caught up. How can anyone get "church" from this verse? This verse does not line up with the literal verses that describe the Rapture; therefore, Revelation 4:1 cannot be used to symbolically represent the Rapture of the church.

To further support my viewpoint from the Word of God, I will show you that once we are caught up in the clouds, Christ the Son of Man, will lead us to the throne of God. We are not "caught up" to the throne. I think you will get my point if you read the vision of Daniel.

In Daniel 7:13 it says, *In my vision at night, I looked, and there before me was one like the son of man, coming with the clouds of heaven. He approached the Ancient of Days and was led into his presence.* As you study the rest of Daniel 7, you will see that the saints are released from the grasp of the antichrist and are given the Kingdom. This time when the saints are allowed to possess the Kingdom is the same time as the Rapture because it goes on to say that the amount of time the antichrist was making war on the saints was three and one-half years. This shows the Rapture taking place in the middle of the Great Tribulation. Read Daniel 7:21-22: ***As I watched, this horn was waging war against the saints and defeating them, until the Ancient of Days came and pronounced judgment in favor of the saints of the Most High, and the time came when they possessed the kingdom.*** Next, read Daniel 7:25. *He will speak against the Most High and oppress his saints and try to change the set times and the laws. **The saints will be handed over to him for a time, times and half a time.** **(Or three and one-half years.)***

What I am saying is the Bible supports a rapture that does not take place until Revelation 7. I will show you several verses in the Bible that show the Rapture happening after the opening of the six seals during the Great Tribulation. First, I want to show you three places from the Gospels that describe almost verbatim what is happening in the opening of the seals of Revelation, chapter six. All three describe what I believe to be the Rapture, happening after the opening of the sixth seal.

I refer you to the following verses:

Matthew 24:4-5: *Jesus answered, "Watch out that no one deceives you. For many will come in my name claiming, 'I am the Christ', and will deceive many....'"* This verse coincides with the first seal about false Christs.

Matthew 24:7: *Nation will rise against nation and kingdom against kingdom.* This coincides with the second seal where wars break out.

Matthew 24:7: *There will be famines and earthquakes in various places.* This coincides with the third seal where famine is the result of war.

Matthew 24:9: *Then you will be handed over to be persecuted and put to death, and you will be hated of all nations because of me.* This coincides with the fifth seal where the saints are martyred for their faith in Christ.

Matthew 24:29: *The sun will be darkened, and the moon will not give its light, the stars will fall from the sky and the heavenly bodies will be shaken.* This coincides with the sixth seal.

Now read Matthew 24: 30-31: ***At that time***, *the sign of the Son of Man will appear in the sky and all the nations of the earth will mourn. They will see the Son of Man coming on the clouds of the sky, with power and great glory, and he will send his angels with a loud trumpet call, and they will gather his elect from the four winds, from one end of the heavens to the other.*

To me, this very clearly describes the events described in Revelation 6. Here you see the opening of the seals, leading up to what I consider the Rapture of the believers in Revelation 7:9. Before looking more closely at Revelation 7 to understand where I see the Rapture of the believers, let us finish looking at scriptures that are found in the other Gospels that describe the same sequence of events leading up to the Rapture that we just read about in Matthew 24.

First, we will look at what the Gospels of Mark and Luke have to say about the Rapture and its timing. I will not write out all the passages, but as you read these chapters, you will understand it is talking about a time of Great Tribulation. There are signs that need to happen before the coming of the Lord and culminate with the Lord's coming in the clouds. Read Mark 13:19-27: *Because those will be days of distress unequaled from the beginning, when God created the world, until now and never to be equaled again. If the Lord had not cut short those days, no one would survive. But for the sake of the elect, whom he has chosen, he has shortened them. At that time, if anyone says to you, 'Look, here is the Christ!' Or 'Look, there he is!' Do not believe it. For false Christs and false prophets will appear and perform signs and miracles to deceive the elect, if that were possible. So be on your guard; I have told you everything ahead of time. But in those days, following that distress, the sun will be darkened, and the moon will not give its light, the stars will fall from the sky and the heavenly bodies will be shaken. **At that time**, men will see the Son of Man coming in the clouds with great power and glory. And he will send his angels and gather his elect from the four winds, from the ends of the earth to the ends of the heavens.*

It is very clear to me that these verses in the book of Mark are talking about the Rapture, and it is the saints, called the elect, who are being raptured. These are not tribulation saints because they are referred to as the elect of God. Think about this: if these spoken about here are the elect of God, then they have to be part of the bride of Christ. If these were tribulation saints, you would have to say that there are two raptures because unless the tribulation saints get raptured, they will miss out on the marriage supper of the Lamb. The Bible does not teach a second rapture for those who are left behind.

If you will read the description of the events that are taking place as described in the Gospels, you will see it is the same as is described in the sixth seal in Revelation 6:12-13: *I watched as he opened the sixth seal. There was a great earthquake. The sun turned black like sackcloth made of goat's hair, the whole moon turned blood red, and the stars in the sky fell to the earth, as late figs drop from a fig tree when it is shaken by a strong wind.*

Now let us look at Luke 21. This chapter almost completely covers the time of the Great Tribulation. What is interesting is it is covering both events that are relevant to the Jews while talking about the events leading up to the saints' rapture at the Lord's return in the clouds. I will pick out three segments that are pertinent to this discussion, and you can study further to verify that I am keeping these verses in their proper context.

Read Luke 21:10-11: *Then he said unto them, "Nation will rise against nation and kingdom against kingdom. There will be great earthquakes, famines and pestilences in various places, and fearful events and great signs from heaven…"* Continue on and read Luke 21:16-17 (NIV): *"You will be betrayed by parents, brothers, relatives and friends, and they will put some of you to death. All men will hate you because of me. But not a hair of your head will perish. By standing firm you will save yourselves."*

Next examine Luke 21:25-28: *There will be signs in the sun, moon, and stars. On the earth, nations will be in anguish and perplexity at the roaring of the sea. Men will faint from terror, apprehensive of what is coming on the world, for the heavenly bodies will be shaken.* **At that time,** *they will see the Son of Man coming in a cloud with power and great glory. When these things begin to take place, stand up and lift up your heads, because your redemption is drawing near.*

This chapter covers all the seals of Revelation 6. Yet it does not describe the Rapture, but it says when these things begin to take place, we are to stand up and lift up our heads, for our redemption is drawing near. When these things happen, why would we want to look up? It is because the Lord's return will be so imminent, we will want to be looking heavenward, expecting the Lord to come in the clouds very soon. Also note, the Son of Man is seen coming in the clouds. This is commonly connected with the Rapture.

Now let us look at what is happening in Revelation 7 (what I call the Rapture of the saints). I believe it is a reasonable interpretation to consider the following as the Rapture instead of Revelation 4:1. Start reading Revelation 7:9-12: *After this, I looked, and there before me was a great multitude that no one could count, from every nation, tribe, people and language, standing before the throne and in front of the Lamb. They were wearing white robes and holding palm branches in their hands. And they cried out in a loud voice: "Salvation belongs to our God, Who sits on the throne and to the Lamb." All the angels were standing around the throne and around the elders and the four living creatures. They fell down on their faces before the throne and worshiped God saying, "Amen, praise and glory and wisdom and thanks and honor and power and strength be to our God forever and ever Amen!"*

Look at verse 9. It says, *A great multitude from every nation, tribe, language, and people were standing before the throne.* Now go down to verse 13 and hear what one of the elders standing there was saying about this: *Then one of the elders asked me. "These in white robes, who are they? And where did they come from?"*

Imagine this picture. One of the elders, who day and night is around the throne of God, suddenly notices millions, uncountable Christians standing around the throne worshiping God, and he did not know from where they came! See the answer in Revelation 7:14: *I answered, "Sir, you know." And he said, "These are they who have come out of the Great Tribulation. They have washed their robes, and made them white in the blood of the Lamb."*

We know these are Christians because their robes have been washed in the blood of the Lamb. My question is, "If these uncountable millions just showed up in heaven after the sixth seal but the Rapture happened in Revelation 4:1 before the Great Tribulation started, then who are these who just showed up? Is there a second rapture for the tribulation saints? I do not see that as scriptural. To me, what we are seeing here is the church going through part of the Great Tribulation until it gets to the part where the 144,000 Jews are sealed to be God's chosen messengers. They are commissioned to preach and reveal the love of Christ to the Jewish nation.

At one point, I believed this looked like the end of the day of the Gentiles and the start of God's plan to reach out to the children of Israel! I now believe there will be a period of overlap between the end of the day of the Gentiles and the time of reaching out to the Jews. I believe God is already working to lead the nation of Israel to Christ in time for the Rapture, as they are to become an important part of Christ's bride.

One argument I have heard against what I have said here is, "This is a second rapture, which is for the Jews." **Why would you have a separate rapture of the Jews when you just had the <u>sealing</u> of the 144,000 Jews to evangelize the Jewish nation?** I believe when the one and only Rapture occurs, millions of Christian Jews will go up in this Rapture; otherwise, they would not be part of the bride of Christ. Furthermore, the two witnesses, who play a part in this, are not even mentioned yet. They are to witness to the Jewish nation for three and one-half years. Also, if you will look at Revelation 7:9, it says these people who have just appeared in heaven came from every nation, tribe, people, and language. The same argument is used here: these are Jews who are living in every nation and speak in every language, but this verse speaks about every <u>people</u>, tribe, nation and language. This verse ties into another verse, which makes for a great deal of excitement. Look at Revelation 5:9. This is where only Jesus was qualified to open the seals, and it says, *You are worthy to take the scroll and to open its seals; because, you were slain and with your blood you purchased men for God from every tribe and language and people and nation.* THIS IS YOU AND ME! THIS IS THE CHURCH THAT CHRIST REDEEMED WITH HIS BLOOD. Now look at Revelation 7:9, and you will see

Christ gathering by the Rapture what He has already purchased with His blood! *After this, I looked and there before me was a great multitude no one could count, from every nation, tribe, people and language.*

Here is where I hope you will pay close attention to what I am going to suggest. I want to take you back to an event between Revelation 4:1 and Revelation 7:11-14. Remember, Revelation 4:1 is the accepted verse for the time of the pre-Tribulation Rapture. Now, look at Revelation 5:11-12: *And behold, and I heard the voice of many angels around the throne and the beasts and the elders: and the number of them was ten thousand times ten thousand and thousands of thousands, saying with a loud voice, "Worthy is the Lamb that was slain to receive power and riches and wisdom and strength, and honor and glory and blessing."* Notice the persons depicted around the throne-- angels, beasts, and elders. There is no mention of saints around the throne. If the church were raptured in Revelation 4:1, then the saints would be around the throne in white robes in Revelation 5. Also, when you read Revelation 7:11-14, notice the elder who is always around the throne, and he asks, *"Who are these in white robes...,"* who have suddenly shown up? The elder answers his own question and says they are the saints who have come out of the Great Tribulation. **If the Rapture had already happened pre-Tribulation in Revelation 4:1,** then the millions of pre-tribulation Christians would have been in white robes around the throne in both Revelation 5 and 7. **They would have blended in with the multitude about whom the elder was asking in Revelation 7:11-14.** Now do you still think there are two raptures? These verses plainly show the Rapture simply could not have happened in Revelation 4:1.

Next, go to 1 Thessalonians 4:15-18. This scripture shows why the Rapture could not have happened until after Revelation 5:11-12: *For this we say unto you by the word of the Lord, that we which are alive and remain unto the coming of the Lord shall not prevent them which are asleep. For the Lord himself shall descend from heaven with a shout, with the voice of the archangel, and with the trump of God: and the dead will rise first. Then we which are alive and remain shall be caught up together with them in the clouds, to meet the Lord in the air, and so shall we ever be with the Lord, wherefore comfort one another with these words.*

This scripture shows why the Rapture could not have happened until after Revelation 5:11-12. Read 1 Thessalonians 4:17. It says both the dead in Christ and those who are alive will both be raptured together to meet the Lord, and it says further, *...And so we will be with the Lord forever.* If from the time of the Rapture we will forever be with the Lord, think about it; we would be with the Lord in Revelation 5:11-12 around the throne. If there is no mention of saints in white robes around the throne in Revelation 5:11-12, then the Rapture has not yet happened. However, when the elder in Revelation 7: 9-14 asks, *"Who are these multitudes in white robes **which no man can number?**"* he answers himself by saying, *"These are they who have come out of the Great Tribulation."* On the other hand, **those in Revelation 5:11-12 ARE numbered!** Can it be any clearer? The Rapture, the only Rapture, has just taken place in Revelation 7:11-14.

Another argument says that those who have suddenly appeared around the throne in Revelation 7:9 are the martyred saints. However, based on the reaction of the elder, what happened here happened suddenly! The fact that the elder asking the question is always at the throne proves it. It is as if he blinked, and all of a sudden, there are millions in white robes around the throne. This would mean if they were Great Tribulation martyred saints, they would have had to be killed at the same time. I do not think this is possible. Remember, it says the number of them could not be numbered! In Revelation 5:11, when angelic beings were worshiping around the throne, the numbers were in the millions, but when those in white robes appear, it says in Revelation 7:9: *After this I looked and there before me was a great multitude that no one could count.*

There is a second problem with the above interpretation. When the saints are being martyred, as described in the fifth seal in Revelation 6:9-10, it says the martyred saints are <u>under</u> the altar, not "...at the throne." And they are asking, *"How long until you avenge our blood?"*

Then it says they were each given white robes. They are still <u>under</u> the altar, not at the throne. If these martyred saints were at the throne in Revelation 6:10 in the white robes given to them while <u>under</u> the altar, the elder in Revelation 7 would not have even noticed a second multitude showing up, for over the last two thousand years, millions of Christians have been martyred. At the Rapture, they would all have been at the throne. **Now think about this: if all the martyred saints of all time do not show up at the throne until Revelation 7, how can anyone say the Rapture happened in Revelation 4:1?**

When you look at what I have covered, concerning whether or not Revelation 4:1 discusses the Rapture, the lion's share of scripture shows this interpretation to be very weak.

4. The church is not mentioned after Revelation 4:1.

The fourth argument for the pre-tribulation position of the Rapture concerns the word "church". Because the word "church" is not mentioned after Revelation 4:1, it is taught that the church was raptured and is no longer on the earth.

My first response to this argument is that this is untrue. The scriptures say the saints would be martyred during the fifth seal of the Great Tribulation in Revelation 6. Then again, in Revelation 14:11-13, the Bible talks of those who are taking the mark of the beast and the needed patience of the saints during this time. It goes on to say many saints will be martyred at this time. Now I know there are some who teach those saints are tribulation saints. Tell me, where are the words, "tribulation saints," in the Bible? Plus, realize we are setting the time of the Rapture as pre-Tribulation not based on scripture verses but based on the omission of the word "church" after Revelation 4:1. Not only are we basing the timing of the Rapture on the omission of "church", but we are interpreting Revelation 4:1 with a symbolic meaning to make it mean whatever it has to mean to support a pre-tribulation rapture.

As I see it, the timing of the Rapture is too important to establish this doctrine without clearly stating scripture, chapter and verse to back it up. In addition, think about this, what is the church? It is the saints that make the church, so if the saints are mentioned after Revelation chapter 4:1, then the church is mentioned. Furthermore, if you study Daniel's vision found in Daniel 7, you will see he speaks about the Rapture of the saints taking place in his vision, and there is no mention of the church. It only talks about the saints. I will go into greater detail about the Rapture teaching found in Daniel in the following chapter.

Another point I would like to make concerning the argument that there is no mention of the church after Revelation 4:1 is that in order for this statement to be accurate, it would have to be true for the whole Bible and not just the book of Revelation. If the CHURCH is mentioned in any other book of the Bible in reference to the church going through the Great Tribulation, then this argument does not hold up. I believe 2 Thessalonians shows the church going through the Great Tribulation, and it is plainly worded without drawing a conclusion based on symbolism.

Read 2 Thessalonians 1:4-10. *Therefore, among God's CHURCHES, we boast about your perseverance and faith in all the persecutions and trials you are enduring. All this is evidence that God's judgment is right, and as a result you will be counted worthy of the kingdom of God, for which you are suffering. God is just: He will pay back trouble to those who trouble you and give relief to you who are troubled, and to us as well. This will happen when the Lord Jesus is revealed from heaven in blazing fire with his powerful angels. He will punish those who do not know God and do not obey the gospel of our Lord Jesus. They will be punished with everlasting destruction and shut out from the presence of the Lord and from the majesty of his power on the day he comes to be glorified in his holy people and to be marveled at among all those who have believed. This includes you because you believed our testimony to you.*

If you will continue reading 2 Thessalonians 2, you will see it is undeniable these chapters concern the time of the Great Tribulation leading up to the Lord's return, the time when Christ returns to put down all evil. Chapter 2 continues to make reference to the time of the antichrist, and 2 Thessalonians 2:1-3 specifically refers to the gathering to Christ, or the Rapture, as not occurring until some point after the antichrist arrives.

If this is where I were to stop and say that it is not a strong argument for a pre-tribulation rapture just because the church is not mentioned after Revelation 4:1, I would have been content. Many times during this study, I have felt the Holy Spirit prompting me to look deeper into His Word through what I would call spontaneous promptings of the Holy Spirit. What I have to share now comes from one of those promptings. I only say this because I know I could not have written this book without the help of the Holy Spirit, and I will not take credit that belongs to God.

I was prompted to study all references concerning the Rapture of the church, with the thought that the Bible does not teach that Christ is coming back for the church. My first thought was, "Could it be the Bible does not teach Christ is coming back for the church?" With that thought in mind, I opened my Strong's concordance and looked up every reference to church in the Bible. The church is mentioned eighty times. I looked up "saints," and "saints" is mentioned ninety-six times. What immediately jumped out at me was there is not one single mention of Christ coming back for the church.

There is no mention of the church in heaven, and, in fact, if you will read the following verses, you will see it is the saints for whom Christ is coming back. It is the saints who will rule with Christ in the ages to come.

Daniel 7:18: *But the saints of the Most High will receive the kingdom and will possess it forever – yes, forever and forever.*

Zechariah 14:5 (KJV): *....and the Lord my God shall come, and all the saints with thee.*

1 Corinthians 6:2: *Do you not know that the saints will judge the world....*

1 Thessalonians 3:13 (KJV): *....at the coming of our Lord Jesus Christ with all his saints.*

Jude 14 (KJV): *And Enoch also the seventh from Adam, prophesied of these, saying, Behold the Lord cometh with ten thousands of his saints.*

In order to get a good handle on what I discovered, I had to ask myself, "Who or what is the church?" It is a given the church is not a building. A building only provides the saints a place to come together to worship and serve God.

So who are these who come together to make up the church? I call them the collection of all those who identify themselves as Christians, as children of God or believers. **We must realize not everyone who calls himself a Christian is or will be saved.** The Bible says even Satan believes in God, and we know he will not have a home in heaven.

Read Revelation 2 and 3 about the seven churches of Revelation. Interestingly, none of the churches were perfect. Some were better than others, but without exception each description of the churches ended with the statement, ***To him who overcomes would receive a reward.*** **This leads me to say that Christ is not coming back for the church but for the overcomer. How does God's Word describe who the overcomers are? They are referred to as the saints or the elect. So, it is noted that the word "church" is not mentioned after Revelation 4:1, resulting in the assumption that the church was raptured. This is not the case! There is not a single mention in the Bible that Jesus Christ is coming back for the church. No, Christ is coming back for his elect, the saints. The fact that the church is not mentioned after Revelation 4:1 is irrelevant.** I believe it makes more sense to say the church age is over after Revelation 4:1, for nowhere in God's Word does it describe the church going to heaven. No, only individual children of God will go to heaven, and those children are the saints.

In closing, the saints are mentioned after Revelation 4:1 because the

Rapture has not yet happened. In fact, the Rapture is described in both Revelation 7 and 14, and the saints are mentioned in the context of this event. In the next chapter, I present a study in Daniel, and I will show how God's Word clearly describes the Rapture, showing this most important event happening in the middle of the Great Tribulation.

— CHAPTER TEN —

MID-TRIBULATION RAPTURE?
I MAKE MY CASE.

This chapter has three parts. First, I will cover seven Bible-backed events that must take place in the last generation before the Rapture can happen. Only one of these events has happened to date.

Second, I will do a study from the book of Daniel that clearly shows that the Rapture will be a mid-tribulation event.

Third, I will present the teaching from my timeline chart showing a mid-tribulation Rapture.

Along with the teaching of a pre-tribulation rapture has been the teaching of the imminent return of the Lord regarding the Rapture. As I show in chapter seven, "Other Bible Teachers' Perspectives Concerning the Rapture," many pre-tribulation rapture teachers have taught that the timing of the Rapture has been imminent for almost two thousand years! I was discussing this point with one pastor friend and told him, "How could the Rapture have been imminent for even one hundred years if Israel had not been reborn as a nation until 1948?" His response was, "Well, now it is imminent." Below I will show six events that can be shown from scripture that must take place before the Rapture.

PART ONE:

SIX EVENTS THAT MUST TAKE PLACE BEFORE THE RAPTURE CAN OCCUR.

When I started this study, there was one verse that convinced me that the Rapture was not an imminent event. After over three years of working on this study, I believe with the help of the Holy Spirit, I now see that from the time of the rebirth of Israel, (the event that triggers the beginning of the last generation before the return of the Lord Jesus), there are at least seven events that must happen before the Rapture of the believers. Only one of these scripturally supported events has been fulfilled. That is the rebirth of Israel in 1948. You may want to go back and review this study concerning the rebirth of Israel in 1948 from my book's introduction. Below, I will go over the remaining six events that must take place before the Rapture can occur.

1. The one-world government must be in place before the Rapture can occur.

To avoid redundancy, I must encourage you to review chapter eight, "The Coming Antichrist." This chapter clearly shows from God's Word that before the antichrist can be revealed, the ten leaders, or as I call them, "the ten heads of state," and the one-world government must be in place before the Rapture can occur. (The antichrist cannot arrive until the one-world government is in place.) When we connect this to the following events listed below which show a great falling away, we see the antichrist must be revealed before the Rapture can occur. We then begin to see a sequence of events that must come together before the Rapture.

2. There must be a falling away.

3. The antichrist must be revealed.

As you read the following events that must happen before the Rapture can occur, you realize this is not my opinion; this is the Word of God.

2 Thessalonians 2:1-3: *Concerning the coming of our Lord Jesus Christ and our being gathered to him, we ask you, brothers, not to become easily unsettled or alarmed by some prophecy, report or letter supposed to have come from us, saying that the day of the Lord has already come. Don't let anyone deceive you in any way, for that day will not come until the rebellion occurs and the man of lawlessness is revealed, the man doomed to destruction.*

These verses are talking about the man of lawlessness, the son of perdition or the antichrist, who must come before the day of the Lord or the Rapture can occur. These verses also talk about the rebellion; this is referred to in other translations as a great "falling away." When I discuss my timeline chart, I will go into more detail as to why we will be set up for a great falling away before the coming antichrist even arrives. I have shared in my study in a coming chapter that some sort of global crises is coming; this event must happen to convince the world that the solution to these global problems is a global currency and one-world government. When this crisis arrives, America will experience a total breakdown of society as we know it. Many Christians will believe the Great Tribulation has already started. Many Christians will realize that they were not taught correctly concerning the Rapture, and I believe this will lead large numbers of Christians to leave their faith, causing a great "falling away."

4. The temple must be rebuilt before the Rapture can occur.

5. The antichrist must desecrate the temple before the Rapture can occur.

The following scriptures will show that both the temple must be rebuilt and the antichrist must desecrate the temple before the prophecy of these verses can come to pass. The Bible covers both of these events together.

Mark 13:14, 26, 27: *When you see the abomination that causes desolation standing where it does not belong--let the reader understand--then let those* who are in Judea flee to the mountains. At that time men will see the Son of Man coming in the clouds with great glory. And he will send his angels and gather his elect from the four winds, from the ends of the earth to the ends of the heavens. *This passage refers to the antichrist standing in the temple in verse 14; then verse 27 shows the Rapture following this event.

To give a second witness to God's own words, you should read Matthew 24:15, 30: *So when you see standing in the holy place 'the abomination that causes desolation,' spoken of through the Prophet Daniel—let the reader understand . . . At that time the sign of the Son of Man will appear in the sky, and all the nations of the earth will mourn. They will see the Son of Man coming on the clouds of the sky, with power and great glory.*

These verses show that the Rapture cannot happen until the temple is rebuilt because how can the antichrist stand in a temple and desecrate a temple that has not yet been rebuilt? If you will look up Daniel 9:27, you will see the timing of this desecration of the temple. A more detailed explanation of this is found in chapter fifteen called "A Possible Scenario Story Leading Up to the Rapture." On page 197 with the subtitle of "2017."

6. Heavenly events must also take place before the Rapture occurs.

This is another instance where it is best to let God's Word speak for itself.

Matthew 24:29-31: *Immediately after the distress of those days the sun will be darkened, and the moon will not give its light; the stars will fall from the sky, and the heavenly bodies will be shaken.* **At that time** *the sign of the Son of Man will appear in the sky, and all the nations of the earth will mourn. They will see the Son of Man coming on the clouds of the sky, with power and great glory. And he will send his angels with a loud trumpet call, and they will gather his elect from the four winds, from one end of the heavens to the other.*

Next, read Revelation 6:12-13: *I watched as he opened the sixth seal. There was a great earthquake. The sun turned black like sackcloth made of goat hair, the whole moon turned blood red, and the stars in the sky fell to the earth, as late figs drop from a fig tree when it is shaken by a strong wind.*

As you read these verses, notice they both refer to the stars falling from the sky. These would be meteor showers. The reference in Revelation 6 places this event at the sixth seal, and the reference from Matthew 24 shows the Rapture happening after this event.

Notice all six of these last remaining events occur during a time period that is recognized as happening during the Great Tribulation. When these events that I have just outlined come to pass, it will be the time for us to stand up and look up as God has told us. Luke 21:28: *When these things begin to take place, stand up and lift up your heads, because your redemption is drawing near.* Truly, the last thing that will happen before the Lord returns will be the blowing of the trumpet, or the last trumpet as it is referred to in 1 Corinthians 15:52: *In a flash, in the twinkling of an eye, at the last trumpet. For the trumpet will sound, the dead will be raised imperishable, and we will be changed.*

In chapter 11, I present a study on the last trumpet that goes well with the verse above.

PART TWO:

TIMING OF THE RAPTURE FROM THE BOOK OF DANIEL

In chapter eight, I presented information about the coming of the antichrist. Upon further study, I have found more evidence the Rapture does not happen until the middle of the Great Tribulation. In the first half of Daniel 7, we have the vision of Daniel described and then explained in the second half. I will show parallel links in the New Testament that show the same events. I will conclude by showing you that Daniel's vision not only contains information on the antichrist's war against the saints, but it also shows the deliverance of the saints in the Rapture. Then I will take you on a further study of Daniel that shows beyond all doubt that the Rapture will be a mid-tribulation event. Please maintain an open mind as you proceed in this study. Many people who are reading this cannot believe they have never seen what I am showing plainly written in God's Word.

First, let us read the end of Daniel's vision found in Daniel 7:13-14: *In my vision at night I looked, and there before me was one like a son of man, coming with the clouds of heaven. He approached the Ancient of Days and was led into his presence. He was given authority, glory, and sovereign power; all peoples, nations and men of every language worshiped him. His dominion is an everlasting dominion that will not pass away, and his kingdom is one that will never be destroyed.*

When we read this, we recognize that Jesus is the one who is coming in the clouds. Jesus is coming in the clouds to deliver the saints from the persecution of the antichrist and to take them to His Father's kingdom. Looking further at this verse, you will see it is addressing the Gentiles, not the Jews, as this event is the Rapture of the saints out of all nations of the world. Read Daniel 7:14a: *He was given authority, glory, and sovereign power; all peoples, nations and men of every language worshiped him.* My point will become even clearer as the meaning of Daniel's visions and dreams are explained in the second half of Daniel 7. Read Daniel 7:21-22: *As I watched, this horn was waging war against the saints and defeating them, until the Ancient of Days came and pronounced judgment in favor of the saints of the Most High, and the time came when they possessed the kingdom.* I believe "kingdom" is referring to the kingdom of heaven. For the saints to possess the kingdom of heaven, they have to go to heaven.

I want to show you the parallel of Jesus coming in the clouds for His saints from Matthew 24:29-31: *Immediately after the distress of those days, the sun will be darkened, and the moon will not give its light; the* *stars will fall from the sky, and the heavenly bodies will be shaken. **At that time** the sign of the Son of Man will appear in the sky, and all nations of the earth will mourn. They will see the Son of Man coming on the clouds of the sky, with power and great glory. And he will send his angels with a loud trumpet call, and they will gather his elect from the four winds and from one end of the heavens to the other.*

These verses from Matthew are almost verbatim as those in Mark 13:24-27 and Acts 2:20: *The sun will be turned to darkness and the moon to blood before the coming of the great and glorious day of the Lord.* These events are also seen in Revelation 6 with the opening of the seals. Notice the fifth seal is the martyrdom of the saints, parallel to what is happening in Daniel and described as war on the saints.

Please stay with me, for it is about to get very interesting. For now, I will further link these scriptures to the book of Revelation and Acts. Read Revelation 6:12-13: *I watched as he opened the sixth seal. There was a great earthquake. The sun turned black like sack cloth made of goat hair, the whole moon turned blood red, and the stars in the sky fell to the earth, as late figs drop from a fig tree when shaken by a strong wind.* What is spoken of in Revelation 6:12-13 is the fulfillment of that which Acts 2:20 says must happen before the day of the Lord comes. Acts 2:20: *The sun will be turned into darkness and the moon to blood before the coming of the great and glorious day of the Lord.* Some may ask, "Is the Rapture the day of the Lord?" 2 Peter 3:10 throws light on this, *But the day of the Lord will come like a thief.*

I will show you the arrival of the saints in heaven as described in Daniel 7:13 and Revelation 7:9. First, read Daniel 7:13, 14a: *In my vision at night, I looked, and there before me was one like a son of man, coming with the clouds of heaven. He approached the Ancient of Days and was led into his presence. He was given authority, glory and sovereign power; all peoples, nations and men of every language worshiped him.*

Read Revelation 7:9: *After this I looked and there before me was a great multitude that no one could count, from every nation, tribe, people, and language, standing before the throne and in front of the Lamb. They were wearing white robes and were holding palm branches in their hands.*

To bring these thoughts to their conclusion, I want to share the meaning of Daniel's vision that was given to him in the second half of Daniel 7. First, I want to show the verse in Daniel that describes the antichrist waging war against the saints until God steps in and delivers them. This deliverance is the Rapture that is described as the Son of Man coming in the clouds in Daniel 7:13. It is shown in greater detail in Matthew 24:29-31. Next, read Daniel 7:21: *As I watched, this horn was waging war against the saints and defeating them, until the Ancient of Days came and pronounced judgment in favor of the saints of the Most High, and the time came when they possessed the kingdom.* What is interesting is this oppression or war against the saints has an ending point described in the verse above. It says the horn is waging war against the saints and defeating them until the Ancient of Days steps in to deliver them.

In reading the next verse, you will see how long the saints must endure oppression from the antichrist. Read Daniel 7:25: *He will speak against the Most High and oppress his saints and try to change the set times and the laws. The saints will be handed over to him for a time, times, and half a time.* The margin of my Thompson Study Bible says this time is three and one-half years. Think about this. The antichrist appears on the scene at the opening of the first seal of Revelation 6. The antichrist is not on the earth as the actual antichrist until Satan possesses one of the horns or heads of the beast and brings this head of state back from the dead. Once Satan is this world leader in human form, you can be sure he will lash out against the saints almost immediately. Daniel teaches that the antichrist will broker a seven-year peace with Israel soon after he comes to power. The Bible supports that this is the beginning of the seven-year Great Tribulation. What is interesting is the antichrist will only be able to make war against the saints for three and one-half years, according to Daniel 7:25. Why will the antichrist no longer be able to make war on the saints? Daniel 7:21-22 shows the reason: **God intervenes!** What is the form of this intervention? **Jesus is coming in**

the clouds and raptures the saints! Put these thoughts all together, and you have the Rapture occurring three and one-half years into the Great Tribulation.

This part of my study is very compelling, showing a period of three and a half years of war on the saints, followed by our heavenly Father's intervention. What I will show you now is a parallel verse from Revelation 13:5-6. It confirms this three and a half year period which will end at God's intervention with the Rapture of the saints. Revelation 13:5-6: *The beast was given a mouth to utter proud words and blasphemies and to exercise his authority for forty-two months. He opened his mouth to blaspheme God, and to slander his name and his dwelling place and those who live in heaven. He was given power to make war against the saints and to conquer them. And he was given authority over every tribe, people and language and nation.*

Notice, this verse says he, the antichrist, was given authority for forty-two months. Some have taken this to mean that the antichrist would only appear on the scene for forty-two months. This does not make sense because the antichrist makes a seven-year peace with Israel and breaks it in the middle. This verse is saying the same thing as what Daniel chapter seven is saying. The antichrist has been given authority over the saints for forty-two months, and after that period, just as Daniel 7:21-22 says, God intervenes. *As I watched, this horn was waging war against the saints and defeating them, until the Ancient of Days came and pronounced judgment in favor of the saints of the Most High, and the time came when they possessed the kingdom.*

I believe I have shown a strong case for the Rapture as a mid-tribulation event from the book of Daniel. I will outline below further biblical support from the book of Daniel that shows the Rapture as a mid-tribulation event.

If you read Daniel 12:1-2, you will realize these verses are talking about the time of the Great Tribulation. These verses then describe a deliverance from this time of Great Tribulation. (Notice that Michael the Archangel is standing up and ready to play a part in this coming deliverance.) What is the form of this deliverance that is being referred to? If you will notice who are included in this event, you will realize it must be talking about the Rapture of the saints. Read Daniel 12:1-2: *At that time Michael the great prince who protects your people, will arise. There will be a time of distress such as has not happened from the beginning of nations until then. But at that time your people – everyone whose name is found written in the book – will be delivered. Multitudes who sleep in the dust of the earth will awake: some to everlasting life, others to shame and everlasting contempt.*

When you see the dead in Christ who have their names written in the Book of Life, awakening from the sleep of death, clearly the event described here is the Rapture. Read 1 Thessalonians 4:15-18: *According to the Lord's own word, we tell you that we who are still alive, who are left till the coming of the Lord, will certainly not precede those who have fallen asleep. For the Lord himself will come down from heaven, with a loud command, with the voice of the archangel and the trumpet call of God, and the dead in Christ will rise first. After that, we who are still alive and are left will be caught up with them in the clouds to meet the Lord in the air. And so we will be with the Lord forever. Therefore encourage each other with these words.*

This is a WOW moment for me. When you read above where it says, *For the Lord himself will come down from heaven, with a loud command, with the voice of the archangel...* **Michael is the archangel, one of the top generals in command of the armies of God, and Daniel 12:1 shows Michael getting ready to play his part in the Rapture of all those whose names are written in the Book of Life, who are the elect of God, or the saints.**

It is interesting that after these coming events were described in Daniel 12:1-2, it goes on to say in Daniel 12:4 that these words were to be sealed up until the time of the end. Daniel 12:4: *But you, Daniel, close up and seal the words of the scroll until the time of the end...* Reading further, it gets very interesting as verses 5-7 describe two men standing on both sides of the river talking to a man in linen that was above them. I believe the man in linen was Jesus and the other two may have been Michael the Archangel (and maybe another angel). One of the men or an angel asks the question, *"How long will it be before these astonishing things are fulfilled?"* What are the astonishing things referred to? The things referred to in Daniel 12:1-2 are the time of the Great Tribulation up until the time of the deliverance of God's people whose names are written in the Book of Life, both the living and those who are dead in the Lord. Then the man in linen – whom I believe is Jesus – answers the question and describes this time as *a time, times, and half a time*, (or three and one-half years). This places the Rapture three and one-half years into the Great Tribulation.

Now read Daniel 12:5-8 and see if what I am saying makes sense. Daniel 12:5-8: *Then I Daniel, looked, and there before me stood two others, one on this bank of the river and one on the opposite bank. One of them said to the man clothed in linen, who was above the waters of the river, "How long will it be before these astonishing things are fulfilled?" The man clothed in linen who was above the waters of the river, lifted his right hand and his left hand toward heaven, and I heard him swear by him who lives forever, saying, "It will be for a time, times, and half a time. When the power of the holy people has been finally broken, all these things will be completed."*

Again, notice the last part of the answer from the man in linen. It says that once the power of the holy people has been broken, all these things will be completed. Realize that during this time of the Great Tribulation, the antichrist has been waging war against the saints. About this time, the antichrist will enter the temple and declare that he is God.

Now get the picture of what is happening here. Daniel just had it explained to him how long it would be until these astonishing things would be fulfilled. However, Daniel still does not get the

full picture. So again, he asks another question. The question is not about the fulfillment of the astonishing things but about the outcome of all of these things. Read Daniel 12:8-11: *I heard, but I did not understand. So I asked, "My Lord, what will the outcome of all this be?" He replied, "Go your way, Daniel, because the words are closed up and sealed until the time of the end. Many will be purified, made spotless and refined, but the wicked will continue to be wicked."* ***None of the wicked will understand. From the time that the daily sacrifice is abolished and the abomination that causes desolation is set up, there will be 1290 days.***

This is another revelation moment for me. Daniel has had two questions answered in Daniel 12. The first question concerned the time when the astonishing things would be fulfilled. He was told it would be three and one-half years until the time that the saints would be delivered, coinciding with the antichrist desecrating the temple. Then Daniel asked what the outcome of all this would be. The Kings James Version says, *What shall be the end of these things?* **He was told it will be three and one-half years from the time the daily sacrifice is abolished, the same time that the antichrist is desecrating the temple, until all these things will come to their end. The answers to these two questions have established two things: how long from the beginning of the Great Tribulation to the deliverance of the saints (three and one-half years) and how long from the desecrating of the temple until the end of these things, again (three and a half years). I believe God's Word in Daniel 12 supports my conclusion that the Rapture of the church occurs in the middle of the seven-year Great Tribulation period.**

In closing, consider the question that some will ask, "Is it really that important when the Lord returns? Should not we just be ready?" This is a good question. If the church has been taught that the Rapture will come before the Great Tribulation starts, this gives the church a false sense of security. I have heard pastors say God would not allow His church to go through suffering. Previously in Revelation 14:11-13,

I showed from God's Word that the saints will have to have patient endurance during the Great Tribulation. This will also be the time when the antichrist is pushing his system of the mark of the beast.

If the saints who have expected the pre-tribulation rapture, suddenly realize they are in the Great Tribulation with no warning to prepare for this turbulent time, I believe it will cause many Christians to turn away from God. Some will believe God has abandoned them and that their Christian leaders have misled them. They will then accept the system of the antichrist, rather than starve to death. I believe the events happening today with the world economies on the verge of collapse are setting the world stage to make it easy for the world populations to accept a savior in the form of the antichrist.

We, as believers, have to be the ones looking for the signs of Christ's coming. I am convinced we must prepare for hard times as Joseph did, so when the hard times come, we will be able to take care of the needs of our families and others. We need to be in a position for God to use us for the greatest revival the world has ever seen! If what I have written in this chapter makes sense, I urge you to shout it from the housetops and help spread the message of this book, for the time is short.

PART THREE:
TIMELINE OF EVENTS LEADING TO THE RAPTURE

This timeline of events has what I call three layers, like a three layer cake, that brings us to the same conclusion: the Rapture is a mid-tribulation event. Then I conclude with what I call the "icing on the cake."

The first layer covers the seven events that I discussed earlier in this chapter which the Bible shows must happen before the Rapture can occur. Only one of these events having happened to date and that being the rebirth of Israel in 1948.

The second layer covers the seven seals. I will initially cover only the

TIME LINE OF EVENTS

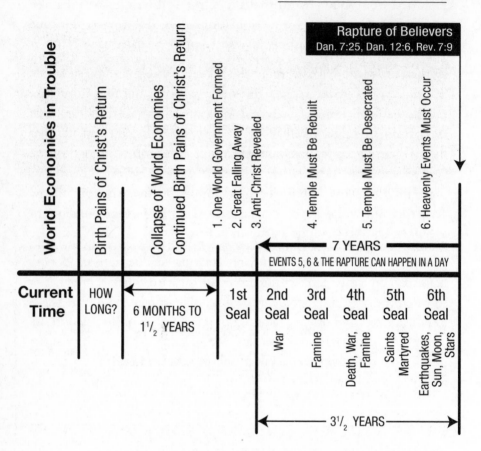

Parallels of Matthew 24 and Revelations 6

first six seals as this will show how this layer intersects with the first layer of my teaching.

The third layer covers the parallels between Matthew 24 and other Gospel accounts with Revelation 6 and the seven seals of Revelation.

You will have to wait until the end to see what the "icing on the cake" covers.

The charts above start with our current situation: global economies are

LEADING TO THE RAPTURE

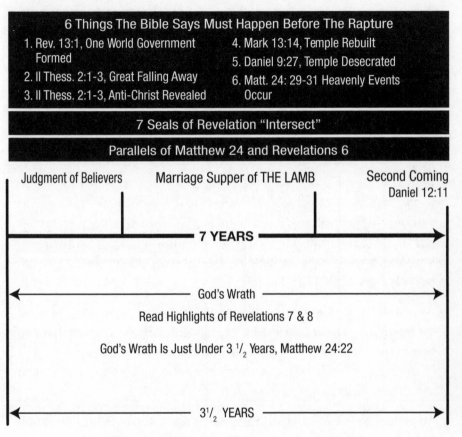

6 Things The Bible Says Must Happen Before The Rapture

1. Rev. 13:1, One World Government Formed
2. II Thess. 2:1-3, Great Falling Away
3. II Thess. 2:1-3, Anti-Christ Revealed
4. Mark 13:14, Temple Rebuilt
5. Daniel 9:27, Temple Desecrated
6. Matt. 24: 29-31 Heavenly Events Occur

7 Seals of Revelation "Intersect"

Parallels of Matthew 24 and Revelations 6

Judgment of Believers   Marriage Supper of THE LAMB   Second Coming
Daniel 12:11

7 YEARS

God's Wrath

Read Highlights of Revelations 7 & 8

God's Wrath Is Just Under 3 $\frac{1}{2}$ Years, Matthew 24:22

$3\frac{1}{2}$ YEARS

Look For "At That Time" After Heavenly Events
Matthew 24:29-30, Mark 13:24-26, Luke 21:25-27

in trouble. The collapse could start in Europe and domino to America or it could start in America and domino to Europe. The truth is the economies of the world are now all tied together. The timing of this collapse is a question mark on my chart. Global economies are so fragile; things could literally fall apart tomorrow. I believe all that is keeping this from happening is the timing of God.

Once the economic collapse happens, within days, life as we know it in America will be over. We will see panic buying of food. Credit cards will no longer work, and what real money you have will have little to no value. We will see riots, anarchy and the institution of martial law. Many Christians will believe the Great Tribulation has begun. The truth is the Great Tribulation cannot start until the antichrist comes to power and that cannot happen until a global one-world government is fully in place. I show on my chart that it could take from six months to a year or more before America will give up its Constitution, Bill of Rights, freedom of speech, freedom of religion and the right to bear arms and join the one world government.

During this time, I believe it will be the greatest opportunity to witness to the lost the world has ever seen. But if we don't see these events coming and get prepared for this time, you won't be able to help your lost friends and family. How can you help minister to the lost if you are a basket case yourself? Remember, God warned Joseph in Egypt, and his preparation saved his family.

As you study my chart, you will see the first layer I present was covered earlier in this chapter under the seven things the Bible says must happen before the Rapture. You may also want to review my chapter on the "Coming Antichrist" as this shows that the one-world government must be in place before the antichrist can arrive.

The next layer of my chart is the seven seals of the book of Revelation 6. I have already given an overview of the first six seals in chapter one, but for the sake of this chart, just looking at the order of the seals will suffice. Notice that the sixth event in my first layer and the 6th seal of Revelation 6 are the same event. The heavenly events from the first layer come from the book of Matthew and the other Gospels and the heavenly events in the second layer of my chart come from the sixth seal of Revelation 6, thus showing the first two layers intersect at this point.

The third layer of my chart draws parallels between Matthew 24 and the other Gospels, and the opening of the seals in Revelation 6. If you will study Matthew 24 and Revelation 6, you will recognize that these two books are covering the same events. Notice Matthew 24 contains almost a complete outline for the seals covered in Revelation 6.

If you will read each of the three Gospel references I show on the third layer of my chart, you will see that each reference shows the sun goes black and the moon will not give its light and then it says, ***At that time** the sign of the Son of Man will appear in the sky.* Matthew 24:29-31: *Immediately after the distress of those days, the sun will be darkened, and the moon will not give its light; the stars will fall from the sky, and heavenly bodies will be shaken.* ***At that time** the sign of the Son of Man will appear in the sky and all the nations of the earth will mourn. They will see the Son of Man coming on the clouds of the sky with power and great glory. And he will send his angels with a loud trumpet call, and they will gather his elect from the four winds, from one end of the heavens to the other.*

Look at Mark 13:24-26 and Luke 21:25-27. Notice the same sequence of events. The sun goes black and the moon will not give its light. Next it says, ***At that time*** the sign of the Son of Man appears in the sky.

Now we need to read about the 6th seal in the book of Revelation and see how it progresses to the Rapture. Revelation 6:12-13: *I watched as he opened the sixth seal. There was a great earthquake. The sun turned black like sackcloth made of goat hair, the whole moon turned blood red, and the stars in the sky fell to earth, as late figs drop from a fig tree when shaken by a strong wind.*

If I am making a good case for the Rapture happening after the opening of the sixth seal, then what I want to propose is that the opening of the seventh seal is the Rapture. Revelation 8:1: *When he opened the seventh seal, there was silence in heaven for about half an hour.* I believe when we arrive in heaven at the time of the Rapture, we will be in awe and all the heavenly beings will be in awe to see the plan of God's redemption unfolding at the throne of God. All will be silent (a holy hush, if you will) until our heavenly Father breaks the silence and welcomes us, the bride of His Son Jesus, to our new home.

In Revelation 7:9 we see the arrival of the saints at the seventh seal. Revelation 7:9, *After this I looked and there before me was a great multitude that no one could count, from every nation, tribe and language, standing before the throne and in front of the Lamb. They were wearing white robes and were holding palm branches in their hands.*

Then one of the elders who is always at the throne of God speaks. Revelation 7:13-14: *Then one of the elders asked me, "These in white robes, who are they and where did they come from?" I answered, "Sir, you know." And he answered, "**These are they who have come out of the great tribulation**; they have washed their robes and made them white in the blood of the Lamb."*

When we go back to the opening of the seventh seal, you will see after all the saints are safe at our heavenly Father's throne, the seven angels are given the seven trumpets and released to deliver the wrath of God to an unrepentant world. Revelation 8:1-2: *When he opened the seventh seal, there was silence in heaven for about half an hour. And I saw the seven angels who stand before God, and to them were given seven trumpets.*

If you will take the time to look up the other Bible verses listed on my chart, I believe you will see the full picture of the Rapture unfold as I have described here.

Now for the "icing on the cake." A proper title would be, "**Darkness Comes Before Deliverance.**" As I already pointed out, there are three separate accounts in the Gospels showing that when the sun goes dark, **at that time** *the sign of the Son of Man will appear in the clouds.* When the sun goes dark, we can truly look up, for our redemption draweth near.

If we turn to the book of Exodus, we will see the account of Moses getting ready to lead God's people to freedom. The last plague before the plague of the firstborn was darkness. Exodus 10:21: *Then the Lord said to Moses, "Stretch out your hand toward the sky so that darkness will spread over Egypt, darkness that can be felt."* When Moses did as God instructed, it was dark for three days. This was the last plaque before deliverance. Following the darkness was the plaque of the first born. This event was deliverance for God's children who were under the blood. But it was judgment for those who were not under the blood.

If we go to the cross just before Jesus died, it was dark for three hours. Mark 15:33: *At the sixth hour darkness came over the whole land until the ninth hour.* Then we read a further account of the crucifixion found in John 19:30. *When he had received the drink. Jesus said, "It is finished." With that he bowed his head and gave up his spirit.* At the Crucifixion, it was dark for three hours before Jesus died, and we were delivered from sin.

Next are the events at the end of the sixth seal. Matthew 24:29-31, *Immediately after the distress of those days, the sun will be darkened and the moon will not give its light: the stars will fall from the sky, and the heavenly bodies will be shaken.* **At that time** *the sign of the son of man will appear in the sky, and all the nations of the earth will mourn. They will see the Son of Man coming on the clouds of the sky, with power and great glory. And he will send his angels with a loud trumpet call, and they will gather his elect from the four winds, from one end of the heavens to the other.* What does "**At that time**" mean? It's obvious to me. It means when the sun goes black and the moon does not give its light. "**At that time**" is the Rapture.

I will share one last verse from the Old Testament showing the Rapture after the darkness. Joel 2:30-31: *I will show wonders in the heavens and on the earth, blood and fire and billows of smoke. The sun will be turned into darkness and the moon to blood before the coming of the great and dreadful day of the Lord.* There are three key points to look at in these verses. Points one and two are from the verse that says *the great and dreadful day.* It will be great for God's people and dreadful for the unrepentant. Go back to the sixth seal of Revelation 6 where it says *The sun turned black like sackcloth made of goat hair.* This is the part of the sixth seal that causes us, the redeemed, to rejoice. When you go down a bit further, you will see where it is a dreadful day for the unrepentant. Revelations 6:14-17, *The sky receded like a scroll rolling up, and every mountain and island was removed from its place. Then the kings of the earth, the princes, the generals, the rich, the mighty, and every slave and every free man hid in caves and among the rocks of the mountains. "Fall on us and hide us from the face of him who sits on the throne and from the wrath of the Lamb! For the great day of their wrath has come, and who can stand."* This excites me. We have just been delivered from harm's way, the war on the saints is over, and we are about to be welcomed by our heavenly Father as Jesus leads His bride to the throne to meet Him.

The last point of interest in this verse in Joel 2:30-31 is the phrase, "Day of the Lord." This phrase, "Day of the Lord," is often referenced in the Bible as the time of the Rapture.

I have made my case. Now I ask you, the reader, to examine the scriptures to see if what I am presenting is sound.

— CHAPTER ELEVEN —

POST-TRIBULATION VIEW
OF THE RAPTURE

In my studies, I have read that five to ten percent of Christians believe the Rapture will not happen until the end of the Great Tribulation. I was not going to cover this viewpoint in my book because I have always believed this position is indefensible. If you keep the integrity of God's Word, I do not believe you can defend a doctrinal position that contradicts other portions of God's Word. God's Word will not contradict itself. When I decided to cover this position, I decided I would pick the two most commonly used scriptural arguments in favor of the post-tribulation view and show why this position is flawed.

One of the arguments for the post-tribulation position found in God's Word is in 1 Corinthians 15:52: *In a flash, in the twinkling of an eye, at the last trumpet, for the trumpet will sound, the dead will be raised imperishable, and we will be changed.* Some who hold to the post-tribulation view will say there is only one last trumpet found in the Bible, which is the last trumpet of the seven trumpets of God's wrath found in the book of Revelation. One problem I see with using this verse for the post-tribulation position is the last trumpet of the seven trumpets of God's wrath still leaves the seven bowls of God's wrath to come. This would mean the Rapture occurs in the middle of God's wrath, not at the end of God's wrath.

In addition, read the reference in Revelation that has the last trumpet contained in it. Revelation 11:15: *The seventh angel sounded his trumpet, and there were loud voices in heaven which said, "The kingdom of the world has become the Kingdom of our Lord and of his Christ. And he will reign forever and ever."* This verse gives no hint of the Rapture having just taken place. It sounds like the victory over evil has been won. This does not sound like a rapture verse. If you could say this verse sounds as if the Rapture has just taken place, then you would have a serious problem keeping the integrity of God's Word, for as I have said, God's Word will not contradict itself. Take a look at 1 Thessalonians 1:10, and you will find a major contradiction: *And to wait for his Son from heaven, whom he raised from the dead - Jesus who rescues us from the coming wrath.* Then read 1 Thessalonians 5:9: *For God did not appoint us to suffer wrath but to receive Salvation through our Lord Jesus Christ.*

The Word of God clearly shows we will not be on earth when the wrath of God is happening. If you read these chapters in the Bible which contain the verses I am using, they show we will not experience the wrath of God. You will see both of these chapters are talking about the coming of the Lord and the Rapture. I know some will say God can protect us in the midst of His wrath, but if you study the wrath of God, you will see vast areas of the earth are destroyed. When the fifth trumpet of God's wrath is delivered, the scorpion creatures are released. It only says they are not to touch the 144,000 sealed Jews who were from the twelve tribes of Israel. **Why is there no provision for the saints to be untouched by the scorpion creatures? It is simple. The saints are not on the earth; they have been raptured before the wrath of God starts.**

I do not believe there is a contradiction in the Word of God that cannot be explained if you study and look for an explanation. Follow along as I present an alternative explanation concerning the last trumpet. I believe you will see it makes a lot of sense.

When the book of 1 Corinthians was written, the book of Revelation did not exist. In fact, it could have been forty more years before the aged Apostle John wrote the book of Revelation. I know it could be possible for God to reference a book that is not yet written, but we are dealing with a contradiction that compels us to look for an alternative explanation from God's Word.

A STUDY OF THE LAST TRUMPET

Those, who believe in a post-tribulation rapture based on the last trumpet, say there is only one last trumpet found in the Bible, namely in the book of Revelation. They are not entirely correct. Ask yourself, what would someone reading 1 Corinthians 15:52, when it was first written, have thought this verse was talking about, when it said, *At the last trumpet, for the trumpet will sound, the dead will be raised imperishable and we will be changed?* I believe, from a Jewish mindset, they would have thought it referred to the trumpets of the annual Feast of Trumpets celebrated every year. I have done a study on the Feast of Trumpets, and what I found is very interesting.

A significant reference to the Feast of Trumpets is found in Leviticus 23:23-24: *The Lord said to Moses, say to the Israelites; on the first day of the seventh month you are to have a day of rest, a sacred assembly commemorated with trumpet blasts.* This feast occurs in the seventh month of the Jewish calendar. It falls on the new moon, so the exact day is not known, but it is around the last day of the month of September on our calendar. The shofar, or ram's horn, is blown at different times during this event for the purpose of calling the faithful to repentance and consecration. Interestingly, the Feast of Trumpets is one of three religious festivals that fall in the seventh month. There are a total of seven festivals celebrated throughout the year, and three fall in a one-month period. The first of these three is the Feast of Trumpets, followed by the Day of Atonement and culminating with the Feast of Tabernacles. These three feasts are the only feasts left to be fulfilled in the New Testament. The next feast to be fulfilled is the Feast of Trumpets. I believe it can be shown that this feast will be fulfilled at the Rapture.

These festivals are celebrated as a memorial to past events. The Feast of the Passover in the Old Testament was fulfilled in the New Testament when Jesus, the Lamb of God, died on the cross for our sins. The Feast of Trumpets is a remembrance of God's meeting with Moses on Mount Sinai, the account of which is found in Exodus 19. At that time, God gave Moses the Ten Commandments, establishing the covenant of the Old Testament. If you will follow along with me in the text I will share, you will see a special event happened on the third day. It appears this blast of the trumpet on the third day is the important blast which the Jews were awaiting, for this is the LAST TRUMPET of this celebration.

To prepare for this event on the third day, they were to wash their clothes. It was to be a time of repentance and consecration. On the third day, there were lightning and clouds on the mountain of God, and when the last blast of a series of trumpet blasts went off, Moses was to lead the people to meet with God. It appears this biggest of the blasts was the last and most significant blast of this event. Now read Exodus 19:13b-17: *Only when the ram's horn sounds a long blast, may they go up to the mountain. After Moses had gone down the mountain to the people, he consecrated them, and they washed their clothes. Then he said to the people, "Prepare yourselves for the third day, and abstain from sexual relations." On the morning of the third day, there was thunder and lightning, and a thick cloud formed over the mountain, and a very loud trumpet blast was heard. Everyone in the camp trembled, and then Moses led the people out of the camp to meet with God.*

Think about this: when Christ comes again, we will get new robes washed in the blood of the Lamb. It was on the third day that Christ rose from the dead, and it appears this is the third day of the Feast of Trumpets. Then when we hear the last trumpet, the dead in Christ will rise first, and we who are alive will be raptured. Instead of Moses leading his people to the mountain of God, Jesus will lead us to the presence of our heavenly Father. Note that it mentions that a thick cloud formed over the mountain, and when Jesus comes for His bride, He will be seen coming in the clouds.

When we read Hosea 6:2 (KJV), we see another Old Testament example to this line of thought. *After two days will he revive us: in the third day he will raise us up, and we shall live in his sight.* Then read 1 Corinthians 15:52, and it all fits together. *In a flash, in the twinkling of an eye, at the last trumpet, for the trumpet will sound, the dead will be raised imperishable, and we will be changed.*

I see another problem with tying the last trumpet of 1 Corinthians to the last trumpet of Revelation. How can we be protected from God's wrath and still go through it? A second thought is if we are going through the wrath of God, "Why have a Rapture at all?" I just do not see this verse supporting the post-tribulation view.

In closing my examination of the last trumpet, I did a study to try to determine if the trumpets of the seven trumpets of God's wrath could be different from the trumpet that will sound at the Rapture. First, I need to remind my readers that I have shown good reason to believe the Rapture happens at the opening of the seventh seal. It is after the opening of the seventh seal that the seven angels who stand before God are given the seven trumpets. Revelation 8:2: *And I saw the seven angels who stand before God, and to them were given seven trumpets.*

As I have continued to study the trumpets associated with the trumpet blast at the time of the Rapture, I discovered an interesting fact. The trumpet blast that will sound at the Rapture will be the **trumpet of God,** not the trumpet of an angel. There are two references in the New Testament that show that the last trumpet to announce the Rapture is the **trumpet of God.** Please read the verses below and decide if my conclusion makes sense. 1 Thessalonians 4:16: *For the Lord himself will come down from heaven, with a loud command, with the voice of the archangel and with **the trumpet call of God,** and the dead in Christ will rise first.* Next, read Matthew 24:30, 31: *At that time the* *sign of the Son of Man will appear in the sky, and the nations of the earth will mourn They will see the Son of Man coming on the clouds of the sky, with power and great glory.* **And He will send his angels with a loud trumpet call***, and they will gather his elect from the four winds…*

The second argument, used to support the post-tribulation view, is found in Matthew 24:29-31: *Immediately after the distress of those days, the sun will be darkened, and the moon will not give its light; the stars will fall from the sky, and the heavenly bodies will be shaken. At that time, the sign of the Son of Man will appear in the sky, and the nations of the earth will mourn. They will see the Son of Man coming on the clouds of the sky, with power and great glory. And he will send his angels with a loud trumpet call, and they will gather his elect from the four winds, from one end of heavens to the other.*

Those who believe in the post-tribulation view take the first statement in these verses, *immediately after the distress of those days,* to mean immediately after the end of the seven-year Great Tribulation, then Christ will come for His elect or saints. There are several problems with this interpretation. One is the seven-year Great Tribulation consists of two major parts. There is the pre-wrath portion to the Great Tribulation, and there is the wrath of God portion. I realize some people believe the wrath of God starts with the opening of the seals. I feel I have addressed this topic adequately earlier in this book in chapter nine under the subtitle, "God has not appointed us to wrath." That chapter presents a discussion showing why it is reasonable that the opening of the seals is not the wrath of God set to begin in Revelation 8.

In order to better understand why I do not believe the above argument about the post-tribulation view is correct, we need to figure out where these verses in Matthew 24 line-up with what is happening during the Great Tribulation. If we look at the sixth seal of Revelation, we have to agree there is a match. Read Revelation 6:12-13: *I watched as he opened the sixth seal. There was a great earthquake. The sun turned black like sackcloth made of goat hair, the whole moon turned blood red, and the stars in the sky fell to earth, as late figs drop from a fig tree when shaken by a strong wind.* Now compare this with what is said in Matthew 24:29: *...The sun will be darkened, and the moon will not give its light; the stars will fall from the sky, and the heavenly bodies will be shaken.* Consider this: these two different books of the Bible were written years apart by two different writers, yet they are very similar. When read in full context, they are, in fact, describing the same event. It just makes sense the Rapture will happen after the distress of those days as explained in Revelation 6 before the wrath of God starts in Revelation 8.

This brings up another problem. If we believe the Rapture is a pre-tribulation event, Matthew 24:31 looks to be describing the Rapture, but the timing is not correct for a pre-tribulation rapture. Those who hold to the pre-tribulation view need to come up with an explanation because this looks like a mid-tribulation rapture.

One well-known teacher on the Rapture and the End Times has come up with such an explanation. I will share his view on this topic and show why it fails to fit in with the rest of scripture. In order to explain how this pre-tribulation teacher handles this problem, read Matthew 24:31: *And he will send his angels with a loud trumpet call, and they will gather his elect from the four winds, from one end of the heavens to the other.*

This teacher explains that the elect who are being spoken about here are the Jews and not the Christian church. If we do a study on the elect, we will realize God has called many different people His elect, and in fact, a study will show you His angels are His elect, some individuals are His elect, Christians are His elect, and the Jews are His elect. So what you have to determine is which "elect" is being referred to in Matthew 24:31.

The pre-tribulation teacher I was watching on television explained that when the book of Matthew was written, the church was not formally started; therefore, this verse is addressing the Jewish audience. So, according to him, the elect that are being raptured here are the Jewish remnant survivors of the Great Tribulation. There are a couple of problems with this explanation. The biggest one is when the disciples accepted Christ as their Savior and Messiah, that was the start of the church, and they were all Jews during the formation of the early church. I realize some teachers will say the church was not started until Jesus died on the cross. I do not go along with this because when Jesus was calling His disciples together He was not forming a Jewish synagogue. He was teaching a New Covenant and those who were accepting His teaching were the nucleus of the church. The church was open before the cross; Jesus dying on the cross was the grand opening of the church.

When the Rapture occurs, both Jews and Gentiles who have accepted Christ will go up to be with our Lord. The Jews who will go through the remainder of the Great Tribulation will go through it because they did not accept Jesus as their Lord before the Rapture happened. Think about this: how can the elect, spoken about here, be the Jews who would be raptured off the earth at the end of the sixth seal? There would not be any Jews in Israel for Jesus to come back and save at the battle of Armageddon!

In conclusion, this account of the Rapture is not describing a post-tribulation event because it happens after the opening of the seals before the wrath of God starts. It is too soon to be the post-tribulation rapture.

This description of the Rapture is not a pre-Tribulation Rapture because it happens after the opening of the seals; the Great Tribulation is well under way.

It is not the Rapture of the Jews because they have to be in Israel until the battle of Armageddon, except for those who accept Christ as their Lord. These Jews go up in the same Rapture as the saints.

Now, we only have one other choice: these verses are describing the Rapture of the believers in the <u>middle</u> of the Great Tribulation.

— CHAPTER TWELVE —

A WARNING TO THOSE WHO ADD OR SUBTRACT FROM GOD'S WORD

The Bible gives a warning to anyone who adds to or subtracts from the Word of God and, more specifically, adds to or subtracts from the prophecy of the book of Revelation. Revelation 22:18-19 says, *I warn everyone who hears the words of the prophecy of this book; if anyone adds anything to them, God will add to him the plagues described in this book. And if anyone takes words away from this book of prophecy, God will take away from him his share in the tree of life and in the holy city, which are described in this book.* I think it is interesting God puts this warning in the book of Revelation. It is as if God knew man would struggle to get its interpretation right.

There are rules for proper Bible interpretation, and some are so basic they should never be violated. One of these basic rules is to always take the Word of God in its proper context. What this means is when you are taking a scripture from a book in the Bible, you must look at what is being said before and after the scripture you are using as your text from which to teach or preach. This helps put it in its proper context.

I will give you an example of how a teacher of the Word of God can be guilty of taking away from the Word of God. Read 1 Thessalonians 5:2-3: *For you know very well that the day of the Lord will come like a thief in the night. While people are saying, 'Peace and safety,' destruction will come on them suddenly, as labor pains on a pregnant woman, and they will not escape.* Now this verse is often used to teach that the Rapture will come without warning, and we will not know when the Lord is coming. Also, it is often used to help teach the pre-tribulation position of the Rapture and the imminent return of the Lord. The problem with using this verse in this way is key words are omitted to make a point that is not true. If you look at the next two verses, you will see this scripture is teaching something different. Read 1 Thessalonians 5:4-5: *But you are not in darkness so this day should surprise you like a thief. You are all sons of light and sons of the day. We do not belong to the night or to the darkness.* **By putting these verses in proper context, we learn that those who are living in darkness will be caught like a thief in the night when the Lord returns, but those who are living in the light will not be surprised when the Lord comes back. Those who are in the light should not be caught off-guard. We should be looking for His coming, and when the signs of Christ's coming are happening, it will be time to look up, for the scripture says in Luke 21:28, *Then look up, and lift up your heads; for your redemption is drawing near !***

That was an example of taking away from the Word of God. Now I will show a few examples of adding to God's Word. I will not mention the name of the preacher, but a well-known international preacher and teacher wrote a book on Revelation. In his book, he misquotes Matthew 24:36: *No one knows about that day or hour, not even the angels in heaven, nor the Son, but only the Father.* When he quotes this verse in his book, he says, "No man knows the day, the hour or the year." What he has done is add the word "year," and this changes everything. With the Word of God as God wrote it, when the signs of Christ's coming are happening, we will be able to look up and realize the Lord is coming at any time. We can truly expect His soon appearance. But when we add just this one word, "year," the pre-tribulation view of the Rapture is supported by changing the Word of God. This teaching says we will be raptured imminently, without warning.

Under the teaching of a mid-tribulation view, the Rapture will take place after the six seals of the book of Revelation 6. When these events are happening, the saints will realize it is time for Jesus to return. Even though we will not know the day or the hour, we will be able to know Christ is coming any day now.

Read Luke 21:25-28: *There will be signs in the sun, moon and stars. On the earth, nations will be in anguish and perplexity at the roaring and tossing of the sea. Men will faint from terror, apprehensive of what is coming on the world, for heavenly bodies will be shaken. **At that time** they will see the Son of Man coming in a cloud with power and great glory. When these things begin to take place, stand up and lift up your heads, because your redemption is drawing near.* When the word "year" is added, it gives weight to the pre-tribulation view because we are not to know the year. If the Rapture happens after the sixth seal, this would be a very good indication that the Lord is about to appear.

A second example of adding to God's Word involves what we are taught about the saints. Some people may be taught that saints who are being martyred and going through the time of war on the saints are "**tribulation saints**." The title "tribulation saints" is not in the Bible. In order to teach the pre-tribulation position, we must explain who these saints are that are going through part of the Great Tribulation Adding "tribulation" to "saints" in our teaching infers that these saints were not ready for the Rapture and were left behind to go through the Great Tribulation. Again, when you have to add words to God's Word to strengthen your doctrinal position, you are violating God's command and building your doctrines on a house of cards.

In the book of Daniel, Daniel was told to seal up what he saw until the time of the end. When John the Revelator was writing the book of Revelation, he heard and saw things he was told not to write down. I do not know what he was told not to write, but it is clear from Daniel that some things were not meant to be revealed until the time of the end. Most people say the pre-tribulation Rapture doctrine originated less than two hundred years ago. Some teachers say this teaching goes back to about two hundred years after Christ's death. The truth is the pre-tribulation doctrine did not receive acceptance until around 1830 when John Darby introduced it.

I believe the doctrine of the pre-tribulation Rapture, in spite of how entrenched it is in our doctrines of faith, emerged because of the impatience of people who did not want to wait until the time of the end. With little weight of scripture to back up this teaching, we have insisted we can take a round peg and force it into a square hole. I believe the confusion that will arise from the discovery that the church will not be raptured before the seals of Revelation 6 will lead to mass confusion in the church. Many believers will fall away and follow after the lies of the antichrist; many will be convinced that he is the true God. Read 2 Thessalonians 2:3-4 (KJV): *Let no man deceive you by any means, for that day shall not come except there come a falling away first, and that man of sin be revealed, the son of perdition; who opposed and exalted himself above all that is called God, or that is worshiped; so that he as God sitteth in the Temple of God, showing himself that he is God.*

When this great confusion comes, who will be to blame? I believe the answer can be found in 2 Peter 3. This whole chapter is relevant to what we are studying about concerning the last days and the coming of the Lord for His believers. There are three sections very relevant to what I am saying here. The first is found in 2 Peter 3:3-4: *Knowing this first, that there shall come in the last days scoffers, walking after their own lusts, and saying, where is the promise of his coming? For since the fathers fell asleep, all things continue as they were from the beginning of creation.* **Think about what this verse is saying. Scoffers are taunting believers by saying, "Where is the promise of His coming?" Why would scoffers be saying this? It makes sense to me that when the Great Tribulation starts, the seals are being opened, and the Rapture has not happened, then scoffers and unbelievers will taunt the saints and say, "I thought all you saints were going to disappear and leave us behind, but it appears as if you have been left behind!"**

At this time, Christians will be looking for answers as to why the Rapture has not taken place. As you read further in this chapter, the Lord gives us the answer as to why we are to wait and why He has not yet come back for us. Read 2 Peter 3:9 (KJV): *The Lord is not slack concerning his promise as some men count slackness; but is long-suffering to us-ward, not willing that any should perish, but that all should come to repentance.* Think about what this verse is saying: *The Lord is not slack concerning his promise...* If you read this chapter and the verses on both sides of this verse, you will see he is talking about the promise of His return. **Why would men say the Lord is slack concerning His promise? I believe it is because when the Rapture does not happen according to OUR interpretation of God's Word, we will be complaining to God and asking Him why He has not come to take us out of here.** Then the Lord gives us the answer in this same verse. He goes on to say, ***The Lord is long-suffering to us-ward, not willing that any should perish, but that all should come to repentance. Can it be said any more plainly? The Lord wants to hold off His coming for His bride, the church, or saints until as many as will accept Him do and are saved.***

If we are in God's army and we have been given the Great Commission to preach the Gospel to the world, why would God want to take His army home when the greatest opportunity to win the lost will be during this time? I believe the doctrine of the pre-tribulation Rapture that says, "If you are not ready, one of these days you will be left behind" is a doctrine born by the nature of man. This doctrine would say, "If you do not accept Christ and live right, you will regret it and be left behind." I believe the nature of God, who so loved the world that He gave His only Son so that we could be saved, is a God of grace and love. He is not willing that any should perish. His desire is that all who will, would come to the knowledge of the truth.

If we read further in 2 Peter 3, we see a warning that we need to interpret the Scriptures carefully, or we might make some serious mistakes in establishing our belief system. Read 2 Peter 3:16 (KJV): *As also in all his epistles, speaking in them of things; in which are some things hard to be understood, which they that are unlearned and unstable wrest, as they do also the other Scriptures, unto their own destruction.* This verse tells us that all the epistles or books of the Bible have things which are difficult to understand. In this chapter, Peter has been talking of the Lord's return; so its immediate meaning is that it is hard to understand the meaning of the Word of God concerning the coming of the Lord.

2 Peter 3:16 goes on to say there are those who wrest or interpret the scriptures unto their own destruction. I believe when the saints realize the Rapture is not happening before the tribulation period, confusion will reign, and it will be a destructive event to the church. Many will believe God has abandoned them, and many will fall away from God as warned in 2 Thessalonians 2:1-3 (KJV): *Now we beseech you, brethren, by the coming of our Lord Jesus Christ, and our gathering together unto him, that ye be not soon troubled, neither by spirit, nor by word, nor by letter as from us, as that the day of the Lord is at hand. Let no man deceive you by any means; for that day shall not come, except there come a falling away first, and that man of sin be revealed, the son of perdition.* Can it be said any clearer? The gathering together unto Him is talking about the Rapture. It plainly says this event will not happen until a falling away happens, an event where many saints turn away from God. These verses state that the man of sin, or the antichrist, must first be revealed. This means the Rapture cannot happen until the antichrist is revealed. Yet, I hear it being taught by ministers of the pre-tribulation persuasion, "If you see the antichrist show up, then you have been left behind."

After recently studying the book of Zechariah, much of which concerns the Second Coming of the Lord, I noticed a reference to the prophets who were ashamed of what they had taught. They had been speaking and teaching as if their words were God's Words. Zechariah 13:4-5a: *On that day every prophet will be ashamed of his prophetic vision. He will say, "I am not a prophet."*

To be a teacher of God's Word places a great responsibility on the teacher. I write with fear and trembling, praying for God's guidance in preparing this study on the End Times. I fear many teachers have been careless, inferring what they write is, "Thus saith the Lord." I believe when the truth of the End Times is fully revealed, many teachers and prophets will react similarly to these prophets spoken about in Zechariah 13.

In closing, I believe what the Word of God plainly says, and I will not put my trust in any teaching or in a teacher of the Word of God who cannot back up his teaching with the "plain speak" Word of God.

— CHAPTER THIRTEEN —

CAN WE KNOW WHEN THE LORD IS ACTUALLY COMING?

I do not believe we can know when Christ will return at this time, but I believe once a series of events begins to happen, we can start to figure things out. In Matthew 24:36 it says, *No one knows about that day or hour...* This is the verse that is often quoted to reinforce that **no man knows when the Lord will return. The Bible says,** *No man knows about that day or hour...* **of His return, but it** does not say that we would not know the year.

Look at 1 Thessalonians 5:1-6: *Now brothers about times and dates, we do not need to write you, for you know very well that the day of the Lord will come like a thief in the night. While people are saying, "Peace and safety," destruction will come on them suddenly, as labor pains on a pregnant woman, and they will not escape.* **(Don't stop reading here like many who quote this verse, but read on.)** *But you brothers are not in darkness so that this day should surprise you like a thief. You are all sons of the light and sons of the day. We do not belong to the night or to the darkness, so then let us not be like others who are asleep, but let us be alert and self-controlled.* If I am reading this correctly, the lost and those who are spiritually asleep will not recognize it is getting close to the time for the coming of the Lord. Christians who are awake and watching will see it coming, not the day or the hour, but I believe we will know that this is the time, once it is about to happen!

Let me show you why I believe this. We have all heard the story of Noah. He was told to build an ark and get ready for God's judgment. He worked on the ark for about one hundred years. I imagine he took a lot of ridicule. Imagine hearing something like, "You are as slow as the Second Coming," except they were waiting for the flood. Well, Noah did not know exactly when the flood was coming; he just knew he had to get ready. When he finished the ark, he still did not know the day or the hour of God's judgment, but he was ready. Then something happened that tipped Noah off that the Day of Judgment was at hand. When the animals all started showing up and started filling the ark, this began a chain of events that let Noah know this was the year of the judgment of God. Once the ark was fully loaded with the animals, it was time for the rain.

The Bible says in Matthew 24:36-39: *No one knows about that day or hour, not even the angels in heaven, nor the Son, but only the Father. As it was in the days of Noah, so will it be at the coming of the Son of Man. For in the days before the flood, people were eating and drinking, marrying and giving in marriage, up to the day Noah entered the ark.* This verse is not talking about Noah and his family. This verse is talking about those living in Noah's time that had rejected the Word of God through Noah's preaching. The unrepentant knew nothing about what would happen until the flood came and took them all away. That is how it will be at the coming of the Son of Man. If we go back and read Matthew 24:39-42, it is saying both the sinner and God's people will be going about their day. Then, the Word of God warns the Christian in verse 42 to keep watch, so when the Lord returns, they will not be caught off-guard. Likewise, the owner of a home, if he knew a burglar was coming, would be waiting for him and not be caught off-guard.

Take a close look at this. It says no one knows the day or the hour, but it does not say one will not know the year. As I mentioned before, Noah knew something was up; he was not getting caught unprepared.

He knew it was the time of God's judgment because God sent the animals to be loaded into the ark. Yet, when you read one book written by an international preacher who has written many books on the End Times, he quotes this scripture as saying, "...no man knows the day or the hour or the year..." This is not what the Bible says. It is sad that many Christians have been confused by teachers who are promoting a belief by distorting the real meaning of God's Word.

If we study the opening of the seals in Revelation 6, we see that the first seal concerns the coming of the antichrist. When we see the events described in chapter six, it is as if we are starting a time-clock to the seven years of the Great Tribulation. The Bible teaches that once the antichrist comes to power, he will soon after this make a seven-year peace pact with the nation of Israel. The beginning of this seven years of peace is probably a more accurate time for the start of the Great Tribulation.

The Great Tribulation is described in the book of Daniel in the Old Testament as Daniel's seventieth week. Historically, Daniel's seventy weeks were seventy weeks of years. These years were described in great detail, and history shows all were fulfilled except the last week of years, or the seven year period that is referred to as the Great Tribulation. This seven-year period is laid out in the Bible with great detail. Some events are being described as happening within days from the start of this last seven year period, leading up to the coming of the Lord.

The following point needs to be explained to some who may be confused about the coming of the Lord. The actual coming of the Lord will happen when Jesus Christ returns upon the earth. He literally comes down to the Mount of Olives at the end of the Great Tribulation. There are references to the day of the Lord as being the day of the Rapture. This is illustrated in 1 Thessalonians 5:2-3: *The day of the Lord will come like a thief in the night.* The Bible bears out the event of Christ's coming in the Rapture. The Rapture will not catch us, who are waiting and watching, by surprise like a thief, **but only those who are not watching**

and ready will be surprised. They will be caught unprepared, and Christ's coming will be like a thief in the night for them.

STUDY POINT: Read Revelation 3:2-3 (KJV): *Be watchful and strengthen the things which remain, that are ready to die. For I have not found thy works perfect before God. Remember therefore how thou received and heard, and hold fast and repent. If therefore thou shalt not watch, I will come on thee as a thief, and thou shalt not know what hour I will come upon you.* **This verse is referring to those <u>not</u> ready for Christ's return.** To them, Christ's return is coming as a thief in the night.

STUDY POINT: Read 1 Thessalonians 5:1-6: *Now brothers, about times and dates, we do not need to write to you. For you know very well that the day of the Lord will come like a thief in the night. While people are saying, "Peace and safety,"destruction will come on them suddenly, as labor pains on a pregnant woman, and they will not escape. **But you, brothers, are not in darkness so that day should surprise you like a thief.** You are all sons of the light and sons of the day. We do not belong to the night or the darkness. So then, let us not be like others, who are asleep, but let us be alert and self-controlled.*

The key point to these scripture verses is verse four above, ***But you brothers, are not in darkness so that this day should surprise you like a thief.*** Verse six really nails it: *Let us not be like others, who are asleep, but let us be alert.* The Bible clearly tells us to be alert, watching and waiting for those last day events to unfold. Matthew 24:33 says, *Even so, when you see all these things, you know that it is near, right at the door.* Think about this verse. If we have to wait for these things to happen, it is not imminent, but once they have happened, then it will be imminent. So you ask, what are these things for which we are to wait? Earlier, I explained how the antichrist has to appear first; therefore, this verse above is talking about other things that must happen. What are those things?

Go back up a few verses to Matthew 24:29-31: ***Immediately after the distress of those days**, the sun will be darkened, the moon will not give its light; the stars will fall from the sky, and the heavenly bodies will be shaken.* These verses give a list of things that will happen after the distress of those days. What is the distress of those days that happens before these other things can happen? If you remember, in chapter seven on the coming antichrist, I showed that before the antichrist can come to power, the ten-region one-world government must be in place. And before all the governments of the world will give up their independence, including the United States, we will experience some sort of event that will cause a global economic meltdown. This event will set the stage for the nations of the world to do whatever it requires to bring back order to our world. When the economies of the world collapse, this will certainly be some of the distress of those days.

The Bible also talks about birth pains coming before the return of the Lord. Signs of these birth pains include the increase of many natural disasters around the world, particularly some of the severest earthquakes of modern times in addition to other natural disasters will certainly add to the distress of those days.

As I was reviewing my chapter called, "A Possible Scenario Story Leading Up to the Rapture," a truth about the coming antichrist and his desecration of the temple jumped out at me. I saw that before the Rapture can take place, the temple has to be rebuilt. I could not believe what I saw in God's Word, but it is there. The rebuilding of the temple is just another sign of Christ's return.

In closing this point, I believe we need to be watching and waiting for these events and preparing for what will happen before this time. I believe these events will shake up our world, and before the Rapture, we will see the greatest revival the world has ever seen! These will be trying days, and we need to be ready to share the gospel with the lost who will be coming back to God and turning to Christians, looking for answers to what is happening in our world. If we realize the Lord's coming is soon, we can prepare to reach out to the lost and even to the Christians who are confused and offer them hope and assistance during these troubling times.

Concerning our knowledge of the year of the Lord's return, I would like to share a thought I have had for some time. I wonder if maybe we can look forward to a window of a few years that would make sense for the time-clock of the Tribulation to start ticking. I mentioned at the beginning of this section that I do not believe we can know the year of Christ's return at this time, but if we study the sixth chapter of Revelation regarding the opening of the seals, we will realize these seals mark the beginning of the Great Tribulation. Once the antichrist brokers a seven-year peace with Israel and the Middle East, a seven-year timetable begins, and from thereon in, until the return of Christ to rule and reign on the earth, every event will happen in an orderly, timed, and predictable manner.

For more than one hundred years, people have tried to predict the return of the Lord and have been wrong. I recently heard a pastor say everything has happened, and the Rapture should be upon us any time now. This statement has been worn out, and when the church hears this, they do not even blink. Think about this. If the Rapture was going to happen on a certain month in two years, and you knew that month, it would change your life because suddenly your retirement would not be as important anymore. In fact, a lot of the things we look at as important would suddenly not matter. The most important thing would be telling your friends and family about the coming of the Lord! However, because Christ's return is a big generational question mark, we do not even give this event much thought.

Back in the late eighties, a Christian sect posted billboards and wrote tracts entitled "88 Reasons Why Christ Will Return in '88." They spread them everywhere. They were so convinced it would happen that they sold everything they had and prepared for the coming of the Lord; some sold their homes and used the money to get the word out. Some had their pets put to sleep so that they would not starve when the Rapture occurred. When the Lord did not return as they expected, they were quite embarrassed and scattered to many different churches, starting their Christian lives over again. I am sharing this because I want to talk about one of the points this group and others have used in error to predict the year of the Lord's coming.

Matthew 24:32 talks about the fig tree and the unfolding of end-time events. Many believe this is referring to the rebirth of the nation of Israel. This verse goes on to say, *When you see these things; you know the Lord's coming is near, right at the door.* Matthew 24:34 further states, *I tell you the truth, this generation will certainly not pass away until all these things have happened.* This sect of Christians and many other prophetic teachers over the years have believed the length of a generation, which would not pass away until all these things happened, was the forty-year generation spoken of in the Old Testament. That generation died in the desert after forty years. When you consider that Israel was reborn as a nation in 1948 and add the forty year wilderness generation, this would add up to 1988. There is a real problem with using the forty-year generation in the wilderness because this was a generation under the judgment of God. This story in the Old Testament says those who were under twenty years old were not held accountable for the sins and decisions of their parents. They were not under judgment. But if you were twenty-one years old, in forty years you would die. Think about this: all those who were twenty-one years old in the wilderness would only live to be sixty-one years old. They would die young because their generation was under judgment.

The Bible says it has been accounted to man to live seventy years or more if he is strong. You see, the Bible tells us a generation is not forty but seventy years. If you take the forty years in the wilderness and add in the twenty years for the young who did not have to die, then add in the ten years for those who were sixty and died young, you are now back to the seventy-year generation or lifespan that God said we would live. If you now take the seventy years and add this to 1948, you have

2018. If this Christian sect that believed Christ was coming in 1988 had redone their calculations, it would have been 2018, based on a 70-year generation, but they were thirty years off.

I realize even if these calculations have merit, God does not have to hold to seventy years. The generation could be based on the fact that some live beyond seventy years. This would put things off to a future date. I really hope we have more time to get ready for the beginning of the Great Tribulation. Yet, if during the seven years of the Great Tribulation God is doing everything in a predictable and timely manner, it would make sense to me that He could use the seventy-year generation for the time frame leading to the return of Christ. In the next chapter, I will show many coming events that fit into this coming window of time, illustrating how close we really could be to our Lord's return.

— CHAPTER FOURTEEN —

THE WINDOW OF THE LORD'S RETURN

In this chapter, the thought I would like to explore concerns the prediction of the Lord's return or the start of the Great Tribulation coming during an eight-year window of time from 2012-2020. As we approach the Lord's return, it may be possible to narrow the time down as we see the Great Tribulation actually getting started.

The Bible has predicted the rebirth of Israel along with other events, and one Bible prophecy says that when we see Israel reborn, that generation would not pass away until the return of Christ. I did a study on the rebirth of Israel, showing why 1948 was the fulfillment of the rebirth of Israel, an event predicted in both the Old and New Testaments. In 1948, a window of the Lord's return was opened that was seventy to eighty years wide, the time of a generation. Sixty-four years of that window have been used. The Bible says, *No man knows about that day or the hour of the Lord's return.* However, the Bible also says in Luke 21:25-28, *There will be signs in the sun, moon and stars, on the earth, nations will be in anguish and perplexity at the roaring and tossing of the sea, men will faint from terror, apprehensive of what is coming on the world, for heavenly bodies will be shaken.* **At that time** *they will see the Son of Man coming on a cloud with power and great glory. When these things begin to take place, stand up and lift up your heads, because your redemption is drawing near.*

What is interesting is the number of events of a prophetic nature I have listed in the following pages that are falling into this window of time, 2012 - 2020. Below, I will cover this list of coming events that either are happening or could happen during this window of time.

1. You have heard about the "2012" event that has been in the news about the Mayan calendar. The news media has said the Mayan calendar is predicting the end of the world. After some research, it turns out the calendar is just coming to its end and will reset to start again. Some are trying to say it is tied to solar events that coincide with the ending date of this calendar, but most who have studied this say the Mayans could not have known about these events.

We know as Christians, the world could not come to an end in 2012, for the Bible says there will be one thousand years of peace on the earth after the return of the Lord. If you have watched the movie that was released recently, called, *2012*, it could really put the fear of God in people. Is it not strange that people will believe something like this, but they will not believe the Bible? I believe, as we get closer to this date, many people will be living in great fear. I believe people will take similar steps to what happened as the calendar approached the year 2000, causing the Y2K scare.

If these same people would read the Bible, they would realize it is the coming of the Lord for which they need to be ready. If you read about the last plague that God will pour out on the earth, the last of the bowl judgments, you will see what God has in store as His wrath in judgment for man's wickedness is far worse than what is depicted in the movie *2012*.

Read Revelation 16:17-21: *The seventh angel poured out his bowl into the air, and out of the temple came a loud voice from the throne, saying, 'It is done.' Then there were flashes of lightning, rumblings, peals of thunder and a severe earthquake. No earthquake like it has ever occurred since man has been on the earth, so tremendous was the quake. The great city split into three parts, and the cities of the nations collapsed. God remembered*

Babylon the Great and gave her the cup filled with the wine of the fury of his wrath. Every island fled away and the mountains could not be found. From the sky huge hailstones of about a hundred pounds each, fell upon men. And they cursed God.

If you look at what is described in these verses, you will see it describes the worst earthquake of all time, a quake literally being felt around the world! One great city, that some believe is Babylon, will be split into three parts. The cities of the nations will collapse. Imagine the skyscrapers of every city falling at the same time. Look at what happened to the city of Port de Prince in Haiti. Imagine this happening to cities around the world at the same time. Everyone would be on their own; the death toll would be in the millions. These verses go on to say that every island fled away. If you think about it, most of the islands are volcanic in origin and occur where there are weaknesses in the earth's crust, often where the tectonic plates of the earth come together. This earthquake, which God will use as part of His wrath on the earth, will be so severe that it will be as if every continental plate on the earth is moved out of place at the same time. It goes on to say the islands and the mountains will disappear. Islands are just underwater mountains anyway. This seems impossible; but the truth is if a quake is severe enough and the shaking lasts long enough, it causes the earth to turn into almost a liquid state. Buildings can actually sink into the ground. What is described here does not even mention what will happen with the tidal waves which will be generated by these quakes happening around the world. These tidal waves may have a part in causing the islands of the earth to disappear, almost like being washed off the map.

After this happens, the Bible says the hail will come. The King James Version of the Bible says these hailstones will weigh a talent apiece or about 125 pounds. These will be like bombs falling from heaven. Buildings not destroyed in the quake will be destroyed if hit with these hailstones. Yet the Bible says man will curse God. How can you curse a God you do not believe exists? Well, the truth is, man knows there is a God; they just do not want to obey Him. When God is done, man will have been given every opportunity to repent and will be without excuse when he stands before God on the Judgment Day.

2. A friend sent me a link to a site on the internet that talks about the return of the Lord happening in 2017 based on the year of Jubilee. The year of Jubilee is being calculated to have occurred in 1917, the year England made a decree that the Jews would regain their homeland. Fifty years later in 1967, after winning the Six Day War, Israel regained the city of Jerusalem and other lands that were part of Israel during the time of the Old Testament. The next year of Jubilee will be 2017. By the calculations of some scholars, this is the one hundred and twentieth Year of Jubilee or six thousand years since the creation of man. This would then lead into the one thousand years of peace that will happen after the Lord's Return during the Millennium. Again, this prediction falls into the 2012-2020 window.

3. Solar Flares: There are scientists predicting the next solar maximum will occur in 2012 and 2013. I did extensive research on this, and one article I read said scientists have recently had growing concerns since the National Research Council gave a report, funded by NASA and issued by the National Academy of Sciences, entitled, "Severe Space Weather Events." Scientists were concerned there could be a repeat of the eight-day event that hit America in 1859 called the "Carrington Effect." This was a large solar flare accompanied by a coronal mass ejection, or CME, that threw billions of tons of solar plasma onto the earth's magnetic field, disrupting the early electronics of its day. It basically burned out our telegraph system, even setting some telegraph offices on fire. In more recent years, on March 13, 1989, six million people lost power in Quebec, Canada, after a huge solar flare caused a surge from ground induced currents that turned the lights out for a day. Again, in 2003, it was said we missed the big one, but the solar storm caused satellites to fail, blackouts to occur, and some planes to be re-routed.

These solar storms occur about every eleven years. The next cycle should peak in late 2012 and early 2013. Scientists say a perfectly aligned solar flare could so affect our modern electronics it could take out our way of life for months. A top official from the European Space Agency, space weather-head Mike Hapgood, said, "I don't think the National Academy of Sciences report is scare mongering." He went on to say, "Scientists are conservative by nature, and this group is really thoughtful." He also said, "The NASA report is a fair and balanced report."

On the flip-side of the coin, we have another voice saying the earth is actually very well-protected even if some satellites may not be. One report said when the earth is hit with a solar flare, the alignment of our magnetic field in relation to the sun is affected. Given the right conditions, solar flares could slide past the earth. Even if we do get hit with the big one, solar flares do not create an extinction event.

4. I was recently watching Perry Stone preach a message called, "Cosmic Prophecies in the Sun, Moon, and Stars." He was saying cosmic activity coming on the earth would be announcing the Lord's return. Giving these verses to back up this thought (Revelation 6:12-13, Matthew 24:29, and Joel 3:15), Perry Stone went on to say a certain kind of lunar eclipse will give a blood-red moon effect. He continued by saying these lunar events have coincided with Jewish festivals and with many events that have happened to the nation of Israel in its past history. In closing, he went on to say the eighth time one of these blood-red moon solar events will occur is 2014-2015. Without actually saying it, he was giving the impression that the predicted events of the book of Revelation could be tied to the events on these dates. Again, another prediction of end-time events is happening in the window of 2012-2020.

5. Are we headed for a world economic collapse? While economic leaders are trying to convince the public we have hit bottom and things will be improving shortly, many are not buying this. When the Great Depression hit America and the world in 1929, no one knew it would become so severe until it did. When it looked like things would improve, the next shoe would drop. It basically took four years for the Great Depression to hit bottom in 1933, and it remained there until the Second World War. If we are following the same track, we may not hit bottom until 2012 or 2013. It could even take longer for this depression to hit bottom because we currently have programs in place which take away the sting of a depression for the unemployed. These programs were not in place in the 1930's: welfare, food stamps, and unemployment compensation, to name a few.

We are currently printing and spending money like there is no tomorrow. Many states have run out of the money that is used to pay the unemployed. The longer we postpone hitting the bottom in this economic downturn, the harder we will hit, and the longer it will take to recover. I believe a world economic collapse is irreversible, and I believe the timing of this horrible event will fall in this window of time, 2012-2020. I believe this event will lead to a one-world government.

I was reading a book by David Wilkerson called *The Vision*, written in 1974. So much of what was shared in this book has come to pass, and in light of current events, there was a page in his book that really caught my attention. From page 99, "...the United States of the World is just a world depression away. A collapse of the world monetary system could lead to a world government headed by a global dictator." The premier of Belgium recently said, "The method of international committees has failed. What we need is a person of the highest order of experience, of great authority, of wide influence, of great energy, either a civilian or a military man, no matter what his nationality, who will cut all the red tape, shove all the committees out of the way, wake up all the people, and galvanize all governments into action. Let it come quickly...World anarchy and confusion can ripen this world for an antichrist dictator who will come in the name of peace to end the desperation and lawlessness that will abound."

More than ever, I see the stage is set for a world economic collapse. I believe the economies of the world are so fragile today that it will take very little to trigger a panic that will ripple into an economic collapse around the world. Again, I believe this event could very well happen in the 2012 – 2020 window of time.

6. Another coming event that can play an important role in the prophetic calendar will be the next presidential election in 2012. I am well aware that the printing of this edition will occur after the election of 2012. I have chosen to include these statements and insights in future print runs because I believe these insights may be helpful in our understanding the unfolding of events leading up to the coming of Christ.

It is generally accepted the current administration is trying its hardest to bring the United States into socialism, and this is only one step away from making a move to join the one-world government. The current presidential administration's success with this agenda is very important. The polls are saying this president's agenda is not getting the support it needs to complete his plan, so the question arises whether the president can win re-election in 2012. If he were to lose this next election, the plan to bring America into the fold of socialism and to join a one-world government could be set back for many years.

I have a gut feeling we are approaching the time of the Lord's return, and if everything is coming together, then the question I have is whether this current administration can be taken out of office in 2012. You probably know that a few years ago executive orders were signed into law, by a previous administration, which gives the sitting president certain rights during a time of national emergency. If this is true and if America were thrown into a national emergency situation, the president, without congressional approval, could declare martial law, suspend the rights guaranteed under the Constitution, and delay a national election until things return to normal. I believe if we really are approaching the time-table for the setting up of the one-world government and the system of the antichrist, there will be no stopping these events from happening. I believe a terrorist or an event of nature could happen to allow the current administration to stay in power under these executive orders.

As we are approaching the presidential election, I see three different choices on how this election could play out. I believe that if the president has a prophetic destiny and has to stay in office, somehow he will. So my first imagined scenario involves a terrorist attack on America just before the election which causes the election to be canceled by executive order, thus allowing our current president to stay in office.

Now that we are actually approaching the election, I see the **second** option being the reelection of our president, as a real possibility. Our current president has so many entitlement programs that most who are the recipients of these programs will try to reelect our current president to keep a free lunch on the table.

The third option is that our current president loses the election, but with the current state of the Union, we could be in such a bind that it would not matter who wins the election. The damage to our economy is already done and we are still facing the strong possibility of an economic collapse.

How would each of these three scenarios affect the Lord's coming in my projected window? The first option, a terrorist attack, would be the worst possible scenario. If this scenario happened just before the election, life as we know it will come crashing down in just a matter of weeks. It would cause widespread panic and would not leave the church any time to prepare for what is coming.

The second option involves the reelection of our current president. This could have the positive effect of alerting the church, that in spite of all our prayers and efforts, we could not stop this from happening. It is my prayer that this scenario would wake up the church, and we would have time, before the coming economic collapse to get prepared for these last days and for the harvest of souls. Realize that for us to have a part in this coming harvest, we must be prepared.

The third option would involve our current president losing the election. This option would really surprise me. A new president may be able to slow things down, but I don't believe the coming economic collapse can be stopped. Pat Robertson recently said, he believes we will see a change in presidents, but it will be like changing pilots when the jet is in a nose dive. The real downside to this third option would be that Christians and conservatives would think that we have dodged the bullet, and this could lull the church into thinking that the good old days are coming back. The church would be lulled into a sleep mode that would cause it to be unprepared for what is ahead. Again this coming election is falling into the window of 2012 - 2020.

7. I have given much thought as to whether or not I should include this next event in my book. I initially had a hard time getting good info on this topic until I recently watched a study on television. It was entitled "The Prophecies of the Popes." The program was taught by a highly respected Bible teacher. I have since decided to include this topic in my book, and time will tell if I made a wise choice.

In the twelfth century a Catholic bishop named Saint Malachy, who lived in Ireland, was summoned to Rome. While staying in Rome, it was reported that he had a vision of the future popes. The teacher who presented this study emphasized that these prophecies are certainly not equal to the prophecies of the Bible. Bishop Malachy made predictions concerning all the popes in the future, leading up to the time of Christ's return. This document was lost for three centuries in the Vatican archives, but since its discovery in the fifteenth century, those predictions have been seen to be quite accurate. Saint Malachy predicted that there would be two hundred and sixty-eight popes. The current pope, Pope Benedict, is the two hundred and sixty-seventh. He is in his eighties, and he could easily pass away during the 2012-2020 window of time. Most interesting are the predictions concerning the two hundred and sixty-eighth pope, the last pope before the return of

Christ. It was predicted that he would be known as "Peter the Roman," and this last pope would work with the antichrist. I do not really know what part the pope is to play concerning the antichrist. I know there is one called the false prophet who will work with the antichrist. Could this be the pope? Time will tell.

8. Another event I touched on earlier in this paper that I believe is worthy of being included in the list of events that can fall into the window of 2012 – 2020 is the next big hit on America by Muslim terrorists. I already mentioned the Hiroshima project in which terrorists are planning to set off nuclear bombs in several cities in America at the same time. I hope this never happens, but it is a real threat. Our leaders have warned us it is not a question of *if* but a matter of *when* the next big hit will strike America. In 1993, terrorists attempted to bomb the World Trade Center. They did not succeed, but did they give up? NO! Eight years later they succeeded. It has been nine years since the 911 attack, and they are past due to strike us again. Terrorist groups are constantly feeding us false chatter to keep us spending money on security. Another big hit could easily happen in the next few years, and if that terrorist hit comes while our economy is fragile, it could have a devastating effect on our country and the economies of the world.

9. This next event is one that keeps coming to mind, and I realize I should share my thoughts. It is 2012, and war between the Middle East and Israel has never been more pending in decades. The leader of Iran, Mahmoud Ahmadinejad, is pressing to gain nuclear weapons. He recently addressed the General Assembly of the United Nations and stated that Israel has no roots in the Middle East, and Israel will be eliminated. Another leader in Iran has stated that Israel will be destroyed by the end of 2013. Many believe that Iran will have nuclear bomb capabilities by 2013.

I have been hearing many prophetic teachers saying that the war of Gog and Magog is imminent. I do not agree.

The War of Gog and Magog would mean an all-out assault on Israel with the massive Russian Army assisting the countries of the Middle East. I do not believe the war of Gog and Magog can happen until the middle of the Great Tribulation. I will explain my reasoning, and you can decide if it makes sense or not.

If Israel goes to war in the next few weeks before the presidential election of 2012, this would leave Israel standing alone. We need to remember that the Bible has predicted that Israel will be granted a seven-year peace pact that is set up by the antichrist. This event cannot happen until after the one-world government is put into place. I show this from God's Word in my chapter on the "Coming Antichrist" when I state, "The antichrist cannot come to power until the one-world government is in place." Our current president (in 2012) has already said that the United States will not get involved if Israel goes to war with Iran. Russia, an affirmed ally of Iran, has said that if the United States attacks Iran, they will look on it as an attack on Russia. This would start World War 3.

The countries of the Middle East are well armed with artillery, missiles, and weapons they have not had in past wars with Israel. This convinces me that if a war breaks out now with the United States saying that we will not interfere or help Israel, then this war would be stacked against Israel. With this little nation left alone and cut off from help, it would literally take the intervention of God to stop Israel from being wiped off the map. The Bible says that when the war of Gog and Magog happens God will not only defeat the enemies of Israel, but he will reveal his greatness to the nations of the world.

Read Ezekiel 38:21-22: *I will summon a sword against Gog on all my mountains, declares the Lord. Every man's sword will be against his brother. I will execute judgment upon him with plague and bloodshed; I will pour down torrents of rain, hailstones, and burning sulfur on him and on his troops and on many nations with him. And so I will show my greatness and my holiness, and I will make myself known in the sight of many nations. Then they will know that I am the Lord.*

Now I will explain why this battle cannot happen until around the middle of the Great Tribulation, after the antichrist has made a seven-year peace with Israel. This will cause Israel to put their guard down and rebuild their temple. If this battle happens now before the antichrist shows up, God will have to intervene and the outcome of the battle will open the eyes of Israel and the nations of the world to the fact that God is real, and he will not let harm come to Israel. God's intervention will be proof positive that he will watch the back of Israel. Once God shows himself to Israel in this manner, they will not need to accept a peace covenant with the antichrist because it will be shown that God would not allow Israel to be defeated.

This being said, I believe, if an armed conflict happens, it will be minor and contained. Somehow it will not escalate into a full-blown war. It might take Israel using a nuclear bomb on a single target in the Middle East to convince the rest of the Middle East that a war at this time would be too costly. The bottom line is that the hot bed of the Middle East cannot be put off much longer. The antichrist must show up in the next few years in order to stop this war from happening outside of the timing of God's prophetic Word. Again, what I have outlined here places this event in my "Window of the Lord's Return 2012-2020."

10. I will include an event that does not have a time prediction with it, but it is believed it could fall into the 2012 -2020 window. What is even more interesting about this event is that it could be part of the preparation for God's plan in the Great Tribulation. This event is the Yellowstone Park "Super Volcano." This event was highlighted recently in the movie, *2012*. Anyone can go online and read more about this possible coming event. After studying this, there seems to be a consensus that Yellowstone is not ready to go any time soon; yet, in January of 2010 the activity level had been increasing dramatically. The Yellowstone volcano's rim is about forty miles across with a magma pool the size of Lake Michigan beneath it.

Scientists have been measuring rises in ground surfaces, and bulges are forming in more than one location. The biggest bulge is forming under Yellowstone Lake. Measurements have shown that it has grown one hundred feet in the last few years. Scientists have estimated that this volcano has erupted every six hundred thousand years, and it is 20,000 years past due. Projections suggest an eruption would be catastrophic to the United States. It would cover most of the country with up to three feet of ash. By comparison, the Mount Saint Helen's crater is about two square miles, but the Yellowstone volcano would create a crater of several hundred square miles!

The last eruption of the Yellowstone volcano is estimated to have spewed over eight thousand times the amount of ash as Mount Saint Helen did in 1980. An eruption would ruin the crops across the farm belt of America. A BBC feature on such volcanoes said that after an eruption, "The sky will darken, black rain will fall, and the earth would be plunged into the equivalent of a nuclear winter." The Cascade Volcano Observatory calls the Yellowstone Caldera "...one of the largest and most active volcanoes in the world today."

The recent eruption of a volcano in Iceland caused extensive disruptions in air travel and caused billions of dollars in damages, threatening to put airline companies out of business. The size of the Icelandic volcano is so small compared to Yellowstone that it would be like comparing a marble to a basketball. If you read the following Bible verse, you will see why I believe this event may be what is being described in the Bible. Read Revelation 6:12: *I watched as he opened the sixth seal. There was a great earthquake. The sun turned black like sackcloth made of goat's hair, the whole moon turned blood red.*

One last thought on the Yellowstone volcano from a quote in *Time* magazine by the geologist Paul Doss, who said, "An eruption could very well happen now, for the simple fact that nobody was around the last time it blew. So nobody knows what the warning signs are. There may be sporadic earthquakes, strange geyser patterns or a lifting of the surface, but nobody really knows."

In addition to these coming events that could be pointing to the return of Christ, there are many other events lining up with the prophecies in the Bible that are signs God has given us to let us know it is time to "look up, for our redemption is drawing near."

In conclusion, in the last few years we have seen the coming together of the European Union, often referred to as the Revived Roman Empire, along with a lot of activity toward establishing a one-world government. As a sidebar to the coming one world-government, much has been happening to bring the United States into this alliance of nations. Laws are being signed that are referred to as international laws, and we, as a free country, are now being told we are bound by these laws. These new international laws will take away the rights we are guaranteed under the Constitution of this country. For some reason, our judges and government leaders are not doing a good job of defending our Constitution which they all swore to defend when they took the oath to serve our nation.

I have mentioned laws and executive orders in this book about which I have given very little backup support. I do not want to be accused of promoting fear and conspiracy theories, but I feel I should name two of these laws that are now on the books and share a few features of each. Research for yourself, to see if what I say is true. Laws are being put in place to allow our government to control the masses. The question is, "Why?" I believe the Bible teaches a global one-world government is inevitable. This leads me to believe that these laws are being put in place to reduce resistance from the people when our government decides to join the coming one-world government. If you research the Patriot Act, you will see that our president can declare a national emergency at his discretion, and during this time of national emergency, it would be a felony to possess more than one week's supply of food. If you control the food supply, you control the people. Also the John Warner Defense Authorization Act (already signed into law) allows the president to declare a national emergency at his sole discretion which would tie the hands of Congress for six months before Congress can challenge this declaration. This law allows the president to take control of the National Guard in each state, without the authorization of the governor of each state, and deploy them as he wills. Do not take my word for it. Look it up.

It has been said a one-world government cannot work without the United States being a part of it. One of the leaders behind the coming one-world government has said if the United States dollar and economy collapses, they are prepared to bail us out under the condition that we will suspend our Constitution and come under the unified laws of the new one-world government.

If I were one who believed in conspiracy theories, it would be easy to believe that steps are being taken to cause the American dollar and our economy to collapse. The truth is, our dollar and our economy are sliding in the wrong direction. We are praying for a turn-around, but many believe the fundamentals of our economy are in such trouble, it is only a matter of time before we will see an economic collapse. The question is how long will it take? Some believe it could take a long time. Our economy is so fragile all it would take is another 911 event or a large natural catastrophe to cause enough panic and economic disruption for a speedy collapse of our economy and the way of life that we have known in America. I believe it will be this type of a scenario that will weaken the resolve of Americans to keep our independence, thus making us willing to give in to the pressure of the new world system that will extend a helping hand to us.

A question I have to ask is, "Are two to eight years enough time to get everything in place for the antichrist to show up and for the Great Tribulation to start and for us to see the Rapture of the saints?" My answer is an absolute "yes!" You see, for the last several years, things have been happening in Europe that had to occur to pave the way for the antichrist. I think the biggest event to happen has been the coming together of the European Common Market and the making of a common currency, the euro. This makes all trade in these countries possible in one common currency. This common currency has been growing in importance over the last several years. In fact, since 2002 to the present time, the value of the euro has grown from being worth only eighty-eight cents to being worth as much as one dollar and fifty-seven cents in U.S. dollars. Recently, the euro has been rising and falling. The key point to realize is the world now has a second trade currency waiting in the wings. Up to the present time, the US dollar has been the currency of choice for world trade. In fact, most oil trade and a lot of international trade are done in US dollars. Some countries do not even have their own currency but trade in US dollars.

In the last few years, the United States has been spending money that we do not have. We have also been buying more goods from other countries than what we are selling to them. This creates a huge world trade imbalance with ramifications many Americans do not understand. The bottom line is that this out-of-control spending, huge trade imbalances, and lowering of the interest rates have made the dollar less appealing as a world trading currency! Currently, most of our trading partners are losing money by holding onto US dollars. If any bad economic event were to happen, like a global recession or another 911 event, our trading partners would be pressured into switching to a new global reserve currency.

With the euro falling at this time, some wonder if the European Union will even survive. I believe there are powers working behind the scenes that will do whatever it takes to insure the survival of the EU and a new one-world currency system. Even if the euro is not the future world currency, I believe, in the end, those who are working behind the scenes will look at America as expendable.

This brings up another huge recent event. Up until now, the countries of the Common Market have been using a common currency, but they have been self-governed. I read an article on the internet in 2008 giving reasons why many countries are not switching to the euro as their trading currency. One reason is because the euro is a currency without a country to back it. If the EU countries were to do what the original thirteen US colonies did in 1776 when they drew up a Constitution and became the United States of America, the world would have a new confidence in this new super power to back up their currency. The United States of Europe under the leadership of one leader would give a huge boost to the up-and-coming strength of the euro as a currency and to this new country as a super power.

In 2008, the countries coming together under the umbrella of the Common Market voted on establishing a single leader to rule over the combined European countries. This vote took place, but it needed a unanimous vote to pass. One nation, Ireland, did delay it for awhile, but a year later everyone signed-on. At first, this new power-block nation was voting on a new leader every six months. Now, even this has changed to a permanent leadership position. Currently, they have one country and one leader, leading a new country of over 500 million people. The euro currency is positioning itself to be the new world currency. This new country is already talking about creating a system that will make their currency system a digital currency system. This would require all of its citizens to have a computer chip implanted in their bodies. The technology is already in place, and they are saying that all the citizens of this newly formed country will have this implant sometime between 2012 and 2017. This is another event falling into the window of 2012-2020!

What we are seeing here is no longer the subject of end-time books and predictions we have heard preached so much for the last fifty years. These events are now coming to pass before our very eyes! We are now headed for the completion of the Revived Roman Empire that the Bible predicted would take place before the Lord returns to rule and reign on the earth. Chapter eight, on "The Coming Antichrist," shows why I believe the new one-world government will be in place before the Great Tribulation starts.

After reading about all these things and the signs of the Lord's return just around the corner, **one can see a perfect storm brewing that can rapidly propel the world into the time called the Great Tribulation. Another way to put this is, we are on a collision course to the return of the Lord, and just like the Titanic was unable to steer clear of the icebergs, we will not be able to avoid the forming of a one-world government, the coming of the antichrist, and the coming of the Lord. These are not events that can be stopped through prayer, but they are events for which we need to be prepared! Now is the time to wake up and do all we can to win our lost friends and family! Jesus is coming soon.**

— CHAPTER FIFTEEN —

POSSIBLE SCENARIO STORY LEADING TO THE RAPTURE

The following chapter is a fictitious story outlining how future world events could possibly come together in just a few short years. It illustrates just how close we could be to the Lord's coming.

It is important that you read this chapter after you have read all previous chapters, for so much of what I am writing comes from the studies done in the previous chapters. I will be basing this scenario on scripture as much as possible, but some details will be conjecture on my part based on my study of the Word of God. God has not told me more than what I have found written in His Word. I do not claim to be a prophet and do not want to be stoned for not getting it right. I do believe that God could have given me some help in connecting the dots, but only time will tell if that is the case.

I believe when the Bible says this generation will not pass away until the coming of the Son of Man, it is referring to the rebirth of Israel in 1948. I believe this statement is saying some people of this generation will be living at the time of this event. This could be eighty years from 1948, so that would place the Lord's return somewhere close to 2028. For my conjecture, I am going to use seventy years as the time of this generation. I will be looking at a "Window of the Lord's Return" as being between 2012 - 2020. I could be wrong on the window of time I am using. The Lord's return may happen in the period of time following the years I have chosen, but because of the many coming events I have listed in this book that are falling into this period of time (2012 – 2020), I feel I must use this window.

The start of this scenario will be a few years or so before the beginning of the Great Tribulation leading up to the Rapture, which happens somewhere close to the middle of the Great Tribulation.

I have always believed America has stood in the way of the fulfillment of the end time prophecies because of our strong alliance to Israel. We have blocked and hindered those who have had designs to destroy Israel. I have always believed that something has to happen to change the status quo concerning this relationship or our ability to come to the aid of Israel. My script will be showing how America will be slipping from its position as a world military power and being the world cop, policing those who have stepped out of line.

2010

I will begin by summarizing where we are economically in 2010. America's economy is going on the rocks. The powers that be are trying to convince us that the worst is over, and we are on our way to a recovery. In reality, our real unemployment rate is approaching twenty percent, and we may very well be heading for a period of time that could be far worse than the Great Depression of the 1930's.

When the stock market collapsed in 1929, it took four years before we hit bottom. If this economic upheaval that we are currently experiencing has a similar track, we will not hit bottom until the fall of 2012. With stimulus strategies, the bottom could be postponed a bit further. I see the next shoe dropping between the end of 2010 to early 2011 showing our economy is continuing to erode. It is a fact our economy is very fragile right now, and it is only being held up by degrees of global and domestic confidence. If anything happens to disrupt this weak confidence, the house of cards, holding up our dollar and our economy, could fall in short order.

2011

The American economy is turning downward in spite of all the efforts to turn it around. The year 2011 is turning out to be a year with a record number of natural disasters, both here in America and around the world. Countries everywhere are getting hit with disasters, and they keep turning to America to help them rebuild. The money is running out as our economy continues to slip downward and more deficit spending is stacking up like snow on a mountainside waiting to set off an avalanche of trouble. We see inflation climbing up in many sectors as the Chinese currency gains value. Prices at Wal-Mart have started to skyrocket. Global food crops have been challenged with many crop failures; this is causing the highest food inflation seen in our lifetime. America continues to be challenged by nations that are building up their armies. China, Russia and North Korea continue to flex their military muscles. The United States is using up its stockpiles of armaments, and our military infrastructure continues to wear down.

2012

We are now in 2012. Many people are living in fear and apprehension wondering where this year will lead us. Some people are getting ready for the end of the world like a previous Y2K craze. Food inflation is turning into a lingering problem, yet people are buying and storing food like they just heard a storm was to hit their area. Some people are storing food and supplies based on the predictions of the Mayan calendar. How do you get ready for the end of the world? I am so glad I can put my confidence in the Word of God which teaches that our Lord Jesus is coming back to rule and reign on this earth for a thousand years. After that we can look forward in all confidence to having an eternity with Christ and our loved ones.

Most people believe there is enough unrest for the national election this year to bring about a positive change in the administration. It is now October, 2012, just weeks away from the election, when the United States is hit with a horrible terrorist event. The hit on America was comprised of nuclear suitcase and dirty bombs that are set off in many cities in America and abroad on the same day. A second facet of the attack is biological in nature. A highly infectious agent is spreading across the land. The terrorists have simultaneously hit several cities, and air travel has spread the contagious agent before quarantines could contain it. The loss of life will be great, causing panic as everyone empties the food from store shelves all over America. Schools and businesses are shut down, and food deliveries are coming to a standstill. America is also hit in its water and electrical infrastructure. All this is happening in a forty-eight hour time frame. The hits in America and to our allies abroad are causing global fear and panic. Even the cities not affected by the terrorists are being hit by food shortages, riots and anarchy. This series of events is causing the world to question the future stability of the dollar, and we are seeing the beginning of its collapse. As we approach the national election of 2012, it seems our world is falling apart.

A little known set of presidential executive orders are used to declare martial law in the cities across America. The laws guaranteed in our Constitution are being suspended under the guise of helping to bring order back to America. The general election is postponed under another executive order. With food disruptions nationwide, riots and anarchy are spreading to cities across America. The president calls for our military to come home to help restore order.

The positive news from these events is the churches of America are seeing record attendance. Many churches are witnessing true revival, as both the saints and the unsaved are repenting and seeking God with all their hearts. The eyes of believers have been opened, almost like scales falling from their eyes. The church realizes God is giving us a window to reach the lost unlike any evangelistic opportunity in American history.

God is using the global upheaval to plow the fallow ground and soften the hearts of millions to make them ready to accept the love of God through Jesus Christ. Now is the time for the church to step up to the plate. It is no longer about us; it is about reaching the lost while this window is open. Once the antichrist is revealed, he will quickly move to stop Christians from sharing the love of God. John 9:4 says, *As long as it is day, we must do the work of him who sent me. Night is coming when no one can work.*

2013

We are now at the beginning of 2013. The year 2013 is turning into another year of record-breaking natural disasters. Earthquakes of the highest magnitude are being felt around the world. The world is hit with solar storms that are causing widespread technical blackouts. These solar storms are doing damage to satellites which are causing disasters no one dreamed would happen. One big mess, caused by the solar disruptions of satellites, is happening to the off-shore oil derricks around the world that harvest oil under the ocean. Many are kept in place by GPS technology. This works with computers that control the propulsion units attached to the floating oil derricks. Once the GPS satellites quit working, the derricks start to float off their positions over the oil wells, and the underwater oil pipelines start to snap off. This starts causing multiple oil spills around the world. The blackouts put some metropolitan areas into total darkness for weeks, resulting in great fear. Many people are turning to God. Churches are witnessing record attendance as masses of people, filled with fear, are searching for answers and hope. Governments around the world are coming down on the churches. The church in America realizes the day of corporate worship in a church building may be coming to an end.

When it does not seem things could get worse with the world's economies on the verge of collapse and the United States economy in a shambles, China, Russia, and the Muslim nations abandon the US dollar as their currency of international trade. This causes hyper-inflation in America. It also creates a situation similar to what happened in Germany in the 1920's. The banks there collapsed, and the banks in America are collapsing in the highest numbers in history.

When the collapse of the dollar unfolds, some people who invested in silver and gold are able to turn their investments into inflated dollars and pay off their mortgages and debts. Those who hold onto their silver and gold, thinking it will be their salvation, will discover, once the dollar collapses and the food panic begins, that those who have food do not want gold. Food ends up becoming like gold. Did not the Bible say this would happen? Read Ezekiel 7:19: *They will throw their silver into the streets, and their gold will be an unclean thing. Their silver and gold will not be able to save them in the day of the Lord's wrath. They will not satisfy their hunger or fill their stomachs with it, for it has made them stumble into sin.*

It is during this time, in the first half of 2013, that the European Union is rising as the world's leading super-power; many nations around the world are aligning with the EU, whose leader is calling for change. Things are so bad there is little opposition to the great list of changes being forced on the people of the world.

America's economic and military might are reduced to a fraction of its days of glory. It is during this time, around the end of 2013, that things happen very fast. We have virtually seen the social and economic collapse of America, and we have seen a New World Order rise to power in Europe. It is during these times the governments and people of the earth are ready to accept any solution to these global problems.

Europe has come together to form a one-world government. Even in America, famine and anarchy are so widespread that the masses of people are willing to accept whatever will bring these hard times to an end. During this time ungodly American leaders will sweep the US Constitution under the rug and sign a pact to join the New World Order. The rise of a new one-world government in Europe prompts the saints to wonder who the antichrist is. Many Christians are asking, "Why hasn't the Rapture happened yet?" A key passage to understanding why is 2 Thessalonians 2:1-3: *Concerning the coming of our Lord Jesus Christ and our being gathered to him, we ask you brothers, not to become easily unsettled or alarmed by some prophecy, report or letter supposed to have come from us, saying the day of the Lord has already come. Do not let anyone deceive you in any way, for that day will not come until the rebellion occurs, and the man of lawlessness is revealed, the man doomed to destruction.*

A system of buying and selling is being instituted that encourages everyone to be implanted with a computer chip that will be like having a debit card built into your body. This system is being marketed as the technology that will save the economies of the world. Having this chip implanted starts off as a voluntary program. Under this new system, no one can cheat the government in the payment of taxes. Hard cash will be a thing of the past. Eventually this system will become mandatory, and if you do not receive a chip, you will not be allowed to buy or sell. This computer chip is implanted under your skin, either on your right hand or on your forehead. Along with this implanted chip that is invisible, you are required to have a tattoo to mark you as having submitted to this system of the New World Order. It is during this time the new economic system makes all other currencies of the world worthless. Gold also becomes worthless under this system. All forms of bartering have been outlawed.

2014

Many Christians are wondering if the leader of this New World Government is the antichrist. It is March 2014. There is considerable debate in the church about when the Rapture is to happen, why it has not happened, who the antichrist is, and who is not the antichrist.

News reports hit the internet and within minutes over a billion people are glued to the internet or their television sets. It has just been reported that one of the ten leaders of the New World Order has been fatally wounded in the chest. It is reported that he is not expected to live. He holds on to life by a thread for three days in intensive care; the best doctors in the world are fighting to save this world leader. Then it is announced on the third day that he has died. The news travels around the world in minutes. A special interruption to the news comes across all news media. This world leader is not dead after all. He starts to breathe again, and, miraculously, he comes back from death. His recovery is almost instantaneous. He is being interviewed, and it is apparent to all that something huge is happening. This once wounded leader is now talking about new plans that will bring order to this wounded world. This leader is up from his hospital bed announcing that God has healed him and given him an assignment of bringing salvation to the world and to usher in peace on earth.

One of the first actions he takes to bring about world peace is to broker a seven-year peace between Israel and the countries of the Middle East. This treaty not only calms a global threat to world war, but it allows Israel to rebuild its temple beside the Dome of the Rock.

This leader's charisma and the tone of his voice gives confidence to many who support him and puts fear in the hearts of any who would oppose him. Revelation 13:3-4: *One of the heads of the beast seemed to have had a fatal wound, but the fatal wound had been healed. The whole world was astonished and followed the beast. Men worshiped the dragon because he had given authority to the beast, and they also worshiped the beast and asked, "Who is like the beast? Who can make war against him?"*

Now the antichrist is revealed beyond a shadow of a doubt. Most Christians thought the leader of the new world Order was the antichrist, but as it turned out, the antichrist was one of the ten world leaders under this one-world government. He was wounded and arose as if from the dead on the third day, almost like the resurrection of Christ. Renewed debate ensues. Many are saying that he could not be the antichrist, for he did not have a mortal head wound. Some Christians actually believe that he is some sort of savior sent by God in answer to their prayers.

The first of the seven seals of the Book of Revelation has been opened. Revelation 6:2: *I looked and there before me was a white horse! Its rider held a bow, and he was given a crown, and he rode out as a conqueror bent on conquest.*

This leader is now recognized by most Christians to be the antichrist. The body of Christ recognizes at this time that a system of government is being forced on the world that is the system of the antichrist. Millions of Christians in America are standing together against these coming changes. Christian leaders are raising their voices against these changes that are coming from the pit of hell. A great revival is spreading, while at the same time many weak Christians are falling away and following after the new system of the antichrist that is unfolding around the world.

As the European Union is being consolidated and growing in power, regional and global panic is widespread, and it is during this time period that those in the church, who have been holding to a pre-tribulation rapture, realize the Great Tribulation has begun. It is during this time a change is happening in the hearts of believers around the world. Some Christians are bitter because the Rapture has not happened, but the vast majority realize God has a purpose for our presence on the earth at this time that is greater than our desire to be in heaven.

A great revival is breaking out at a time when persecution is rising; many have their lives turned upside-down. It is during this time all that this world has to offer is being pulled out from under us. Christians realize they must put their trust totally in God. Christians' dependence on God is escalating. Suddenly, the saints recognize it is not about their needs and their lives. It is no longer about me and my needs, but it is about my lost neighbors, my wayward kids, and my grandkids. The believers are learning there is power in prayer and fasting. At a time when food is scarce, people are turning to God and miracles are flowing like a river from the throne of God. Some have said that the

Holy Spirit would be removed during the Great Tribulation; they were so wrong. The world is witnessing the greatest outpouring of the Holy Spirit since the Day of Pentecost.

During this time, the corporate church is under attack. The antichrist has started his war on the saints, and laws are being passed that are forcing many churches to close their doors. Many churches saw the writing on the wall and took steps to move the church underground. Church cell groups have been organized, and believers are now moving into the privacy of their homes. They meet secretly yet continue to see record growth in total numbers. Believers are helping each other, and more miracles are happening now than what happened in the great church buildings now abandoned.

The situation around the world provides an opportunity for which many aggressive nations had been waiting. It is during this time of world chaos that China makes its move to take over Taiwan. North Korea invades South Korea. Russia takes back Georgia, the Ukraine, and other former territories. Other smaller less powerful countries are taking advantage of this time of global confusion and are waging war on weaker neighbors. Anarchy and civil unrest are causing death and destruction in many countries around the world.

At this time Christians realize the second seal has opened. Revelation 6:4: *Then another horse came out, a fiery red one. Its rider was given power to take peace from the earth and to make men slay each other. To him was given a large sword.* With famine and starvation widespread, governments are instituting rationing and trying to turn chaos into order. The world is truly ready for the antichrist to offer the world his plan of salvation and peace.

In close succession Christians realize the third seal has opened. Revelation 6:5-6: *When the Lamb opened the third seal; I heard the third living creature say, Come! I looked, and there before me was a black horse! Its rider was holding a pair of scales in his hand. Then I heard what sounded like a voice among the four living creatures, saying, "A quart of wheat for a day's wages, and three quarts of barley for a day's wages, and do not damage the oil and the wine."* The world's food supplies are running out.

The fourth seal follows close behind the third, as millions are dying around the world. Wars are still widespread, famine is rampant, plagues, and sickness abound. These calamities and wars around the world are affecting one-quarter of the earth's population. Revelation 6:8, *I looked and there before me was a pale horse! Its rider was named Death, and Hades was following close behind him. They were given power over a fourth of the earth to kill by the sword, famine, and plague, and by the wild beasts of the earth.*

2015

It is now 2015. Christian leaders are preaching and speaking out against what is happening. At the same time, more laws are being put in place to silence the voice of reason and the Word of God. Christian leaders are being rounded up, and horrible treatment of believers is happening behind closed doors to those who are being unjustly incarcerated. These attacks on the church start against its leaders and pastors. Soon it spreads to all Christians who are not going along with the new systems setup by the antichrist. During this time, all people living on the earth must be implanted with a computer chip. This system starts as a voluntary system, but now you have few choices. You can choose to have this implanted in your forehead or on your right hand. You are also tattooed with a special mark to let all know that you have submitted to the rule of the antichrist. You cannot buy or sell without having this implant and the mark of the beast. Revelation 13:16 says, *He also forced everyone, small and great, rich and poor, free and slave, to receive a mark on his right hand or on his forehead, so that no one could buy or sell unless he had the mark, which is the name of the beast or the number of his name.*

It is a sad day as the masses around the world are taking the mark of the beast. Those taking the mark are turning in those who are standing against the antichrist. Even brothers and close friends and relatives are turning in those who are refusing the mark. Matthew 10:21-22 says, *Brother will betray brother to death, and a father his child; children will rebel against their parents and have them put to death. All men will hate you because of me, but he who stands firm to the end will be saved.*

The saints now realize the fifth seal has opened. Revelation 6:10-11: *They called out in a loud voice, "How long, Sovereign Lord, holy and true, until you judge the inhabitants of the earth and avenge our blood?" Then each of them was given a white robe, and they were told to wait a little longer, until the number of their fellow servants and brothers who were to be killed as they had been was completed.*

Christians are standing up against the mark of the beast. The antichrist is giving orders to arrest any who refuse to bow to him and take his mark. The numbers being sent to prison camps are so great the camps cannot hold them. Mass trials are being held, truly a kangaroo court, for all are found guilty of being an enemy of the New World Order. What is happening to those deemed guilty is too gruesome to mention, but God is very much on the scene. God's Word says, *I will never leave thee or forsake thee,* and God is giving His saints the grace they need to bear whatever is dealt to them. Read Daniel 11:32-33 (KJV): *And such as do wickedly against the covenant shall he corrupt by flatteries: but the people that know their God shall be strong and do exploits. And they that understand among the people shall instruct many: yet they shall fall by the sword, and by flame, and by captivity, and by spoil, many days.*

2016

It is now 2016. During this time, a period of escalating persecution is unfolding. However, during these trying times, the saints are coming together. The saints are so turned onto God; it is unbelievable. It is like the book of Acts is repeating itself. Every miracle that happened when the church was born is being repeated, but many times over. Angels are releasing saints who are imprisoned. Miracles of provision are common as saints who have food provisions share their food with others. It is as if they cannot give it all away, for God multiplies their provisions. It reminds me of this recent story I watched on the Sid Roth show where God led a lady to take several suitcases full of clothes to African orphanages to help these children. Every time she tried to give the clothes away, more would appear in the suitcases. Finally, after visiting several orphanages, she dumped the suitcases into several garbage bags and left them behind with the orphanage workers. She arrived home and found all her suitcases were full again with children's clothes. This example of God's provision is proof that in the midst of the worst of times, God will show His own He will never leave them or forsake them.

At this time, before the seventh seal is opened, a number of supernatural things start to unfold. The saints begin to realize the Lord's coming for His saints is imminent. Millions are being saved. This is a glorious time to be alive and watch God's hand of mercy gathering in all the lost souls of the earth who will repent and turn to Him. While we realize God's hand of judgment is about to strike the earth, God's Word says, *It is God's will that none should perish but that all would come to the knowledge of the truth.*

God is pulling out all stops to win the lost. This is also the time when angels are appearing in the heavens, proclaiming the gospel to the lost of the earth. When Christ arrived as a baby, angels heralded His coming, and now that He is ready to come again, the angels are back proclaiming His coming and preaching the gospel to the lost. Revelation 14:6-7: *Then I saw another angel flying in midair, and he had the eternal gospel to proclaim to those who live on the earth-to every nation, tribe, language and people. He said in a loud voice, "Fear God and give him glory, because the hour of his judgment has come. Worship him who made the heavens, the earth, and the sea and the springs of water."*

During this time, the hardest hearts of sinners are melting and crying out to God for mercy. Thieves, prostitutes and all kinds of sinners are turning to Christ. What is sad is there are so many church-goers who are turning bitter towards God, instead of drawing closer to Him during these hard times.

During this time, all those on the earth must make their choice. Do they want the meal ticket the antichrist is offering or do they want to press into God and patiently wait for the Lord to take them home? Revelation 13:9-10 says, *He, who has an ear, let him hear. If anyone is to go into captivity, into captivity he will go, if anyone is to be killed with the sword, with the sword he will be killed. This calls for patient endurance and faithfulness on the part of the saints.*

The angels are proclaiming to the lost a last warning for the world to reject the mark of the beast or face eternal judgment. Revelation 14:9-11: *A third angel followed them and said in a loud voice: "If anyone worships the beast and his image and receives his mark on the forehead or on the hand, he too, will drink of the wine of God's fury which has been poured full strength into the cup of his wrath. He will be tormented with burning sulfur in the presence of the holy angels and of the Lamb. And the smoke of their torment rises forever and ever. There is no rest day or night for those who worship the beast and his image, or for anyone who receives the mark of his name."*

These are exciting times. So many lost souls are choosing Jesus over the antichrist. It is a sad time as well because many have not made the right choice and have not taken God seriously. Only God knows the heart of man, and only He will be able to justly sort out those who are ready to go and those who will be left behind. The Word of God is about to be fulfilled. Revelation 3:15-16: *I know your deeds that you are neither cold nor hot, I wish you were either one of the other. So because you are lukewarm, neither hot nor cold, I am about to spit you out of my mouth.*

It is sad so many lukewarm saints do not recognize what is taking place. They have held onto all the world has to offer and will not let go to grasp all God has to offer. Revelation 3:17-19 says, *You say, "I am rich: I have acquired wealth and do not need a thing." But you do not realize that you are wretched, pitiful, poor, blind and naked. I counsel you to buy from me gold refined in the fire, so you can become rich; and white cloths to wear, so you can cover your shameful nakedness, and salve to put on your eyes, so you can see. Those whom I love, I rebuke and discipline, so be earnest and repent.*

Is it not interesting when God was getting ready to pour out His judgment on Sodom and Gomorrah, Abraham interceded for the righteous? But now, in these last days, it is Jesus who is interceding for the unrighteous, and He is using all means at His disposal to evacuate those who belong to Him before the wrath of God falls. In the Old Testament, angels came and ushered the righteous out of harm's way, and now, just before the harvest of the earth, angels are showing up to give the lost sinners one last chance to accept Jesus Christ.

2017

It is now early in 2017. Wow! It is happening! The 144,000 specially chosen Jews are being visited by angels and are given a seal which sets them apart to do a special mission for God. They are also empowered to do this special assignment for God. It is their job to bring the message of Christ to all the Jews around the world. This job would be impossible in these times of world upheaval, except that they are being equipped for the job. The 144,000 are given their resurrected bodies, and they are showing up everywhere, supernaturally. The antichrist cannot stand in their way. The Jews are being led to Christ in great numbers, but, sadly, many Jews are still not yet convinced.

A series of natural disasters start to unfold. It could be called the year the earth shook loose. The next event to take place is unlike any natural disaster to ever hit planet Earth. A series of earthquakes shake the whole earth, almost as if every major fault line on earth had shifted. In America, major earthquakes shake and cause destruction from Los Angeles to Boston. The worst America sees from this series of quakes happens in Yellowstone Park. Scientists reported a large lava lake the size of Lake Michigan lying under parts of three states and Yellowstone Park. These scientists recently warned an eruption was overdue.

In a recent issue of *National Geographic*, they referred to the Yellowstone volcano as a "Super Volcano," saying an eruption could bring death and destruction, covering hundreds of square miles. They were right! It is the ash fallout doing the most damage. It is covering thousands of square miles. The whole breadbasket of America is being covered with several feet of ash in some places and several inches in others. The ash fallout is projected to last for weeks. During this time, the light from the sun is darkened to the point the temperature of the earth has dropped by fifteen degrees. Scientists are saying we will experience what is called a nuclear winter as a result of this event. The crops of wheat, corn, and other grains will certainly be destroyed. This ash is destroying the engines of cars and trucks. Panic and fear is griping America and the world as people realize much of the food crops have been destroyed.

At this time, the saints realize the sixth seal has been opened. Revelation 6:12-14: *I watched as he opened the sixth seal. There was a great earthquake. The sun turned black like sackcloth made of goat hair, the whole moon turned blood red, and the stars in the sky receded like a scroll, and every mountain and island was removed from its place.*

After the Rapture, the 144,000 Jews will be warning the Jews left behind, due to their indecision to accept Christ, to flee to Israel to escape the wrath of God that is coming soon. Jerusalem has been living under a period of peace established by the antichrist. The temple has been under construction and almost completed. The news media has been instructed to ignore any news events of a supernatural nature. The antichrist is trying to keep control of the news. The internet has government filters that make it hard to get the whole truth of what is happening around the world.

Israel has been living during a time of unprecedented peace, a peace that allowed them to rebuild their temple. It seems this period of peace, brokered by the antichrist, may be coming to an end. While Israel had its guard down, their old enemies have been plotting to attack. Ezekiel 38:10-11: *This is what the Sovereign Lord says: On that day thoughts will come into your mind and you will devise an evil scheme. You will say, "I will invade a land of unwalled villages; I will attack a peaceful and unsuspecting people—all of them living without walls and without gates and bars."*

Then it happens; the battle of Gog and Magog breaks out. The might of the Russian army is amassing on all sides, along with many nations who want to see the destruction of Israel. There is no doubt about what is about to happen. In many ways, it is similar to what happened fifty years before when Israel fought the Six-Day War. At that time, the enemies of Israel were very formidable, and it looked like there was little hope for Israel. The United States was taking a hands-off policy under President Johnson. They supplied Israel with armaments but would not send troops or air support. Israel decided their only hope was to launch a preemptive strike against their many enemies. In six days, they had their enemies ready to sign a peace treaty. They had claimed the West Bank, the Golan Heights, and the Gaza Strip, along with the rest of Jerusalem that was still under Arab control. It truly was a year of Jubilee.

Now fifty years later, will this be the next year of Jubilee? Some Bible scholars do believe this year is to be the next year of Jubilee. This battle may determine if they are right. The war of Gog and Magog is about to break out. It is evident the United States will not give support of any kind. Israel recognizes it must reach out for help from another source. The 144,000 Jewish evangelists have told many in Israel that God will deliver them, and their deliverance will not come from the hand of man.

During this time, the two witnesses spoken of in the book of Revelation show up in Jerusalem. What a stir they are making! They are giving a message of hope to Israel, letting them know that the God they serve is bigger than any army in this world and that God's Son, Jesus Christ, is their real Savior. The war breaks out, and the world is watching. Many believe this will be the end of Israel. The saints know the Lord is coming for them soon. Many of the ranks of the saints have been slain by the antichrist, but those who remain are on their knees calling out to God for Israel's deliverance.

There are more than just the troops of Israel's army on the move. The armies of God, led by Michael the Archangel, are pressing an attack that is unseen but very much felt by the Russian army. The Russians are confused, and a spirit of fear permeates their ranks. The panic is such that many thousands of Russian soldiers die in the night at the hands of their comrades. As morning arrives, the armies of Gog and Magog find real reason to fear, as weapons they never dreamed existed are raining destruction on them. In fact, it is such a miraculous defeat that when the battle is over, and as news spreads of the utter destruction of one of the largest armies in the world, tens of thousands of Jews, Muslims and Gentiles around the world are coming to Christ. The antichrist is angry, and he knows his time is short. Read Ezekiel 38:21-2: *I will summon a sword against Gog on all my mountains, declares the Lord. Every man's sword will be against his brother. I will execute judgment upon him with plague and bloodshed; I will pour down torrents of rain, hailstones, and burning sulfur on him and on his troops and on many nations with him. And so I will show my greatness and my holiness, and I will make myself known in the sight of many nations. Then they will know that I am the Lord."* God has opened the eyes of His people Israel, and they are coming to Jesus Christ in great numbers. WOW! Our God reigns!

The work of the 144,000 Jewish evangelists is having tremendous results. Thousands of Jews are accepting Christ as their Messiah. The Rapture is about to happen. It is evident God is harvesting His special chosen people, the Jews, to be a part of the bride of Christ. It is hard to believe after such a display of God's majesty, power, and love for the nation of Israel that many Jews will still reject Christ as their Messiah and will be left behind. When Jesus Christ comes for His bride, those

Jews who have still rejected Him will mourn as they realize they have rejected Christ for the second time! The first time was when Jesus went to the cross for them, and now, when He comes back for them in the Rapture.

Read Matthew 24:29-31: *Immediately after the distress of those days, the sun will be darkened and the moon will not give its light; the stars will fall from the sky, and the heavenly bodies will be shaken.* **At that time the sign of the Son of Man will appear in the sky,** *and all the nations of the earth will mourn. They will see the Son of Man coming on the clouds of the sky, with power and great glory. And he will send his angels with a loud trumpet call, and they will gather his elect from the four winds, from one end of the heavens to the other.*

Now, it is safe to say the Lord's return for His bride is imminent. It is now the week of the Feast of Trumpets. It is the end of September, 2017. The antichrist has waged a relentless war against the saints for three and one-half years. Read Daniel 7:25: *He will speak against the Most High, and oppress his saints and try to change the set times and the laws. The saints will be handed over to him for a time, times and half a time.*

To Satan's frustration, the saints have stood the test, and they have kept the faith. The words of Paul found in 2 Timothy 4:6-8 are so fitting: *For I am already being poured out like a drink offering, and the time has come for my departure. I have fought the good fight, I have finished the race, I have kept the faith. Now there is in store for me the crown of righteousness, which the Lord, the righteous judge, will reward me on that day, and not only me, but also to all who have longed for his appearing.*

The Bible says no one knows the day or the hour of His coming, but the saints feel it is time to look up, for our redemption is drawing near. During the Feast of Trumpets, the children of Israel were to wait for a loud trumpet blast, which would mean it was time for them to be led to the Mountain of God. Read Exodus 19:16-17: *On the morning of the third day there was thunder and lightning, with a thick cloud over the mountain, and a very loud trumpet blast. Everyone in the camp trembled. Then Moses led the people out of the camp to meet with God.*

In the New Testament, it says we are to wait for the last trumpet. It will not matter what we are doing, whether we are asleep in the night or awake when the trumpet sounds. All the saints who are ready and waiting for the Lord's return will hear the trumpet, and in the twinkling of an eye, we will be out of here. Read 1 Thessalonians 4:16-18: *For the Lord himself will come down from heaven, with a loud command, with the voice of the archangel and the trumpet call of God, and the dead in Christ will rise first. After that, we who are still alive and left will be caught up with them in the clouds to meet the Lord in the air. And so we will be with the Lord forever. Therefore encourage each other with these words.* So instead of Moses leading us to meet God at the last trumpet, this time Jesus will come to take his bride to meet His Father in Heaven.

THE AWAITED RAPTURE HAS HAPPENED.

There is no doubt Israel and all of God's chosen elect have come out on top after this battle, but the antichrist is about to launch his next attack against Israel. God has just removed His saints from the reach of the antichrist, and the new temple has been rebuilt and dedicated in Jerusalem. After the battle of Gog and Magog, the antichrist shows up and visits the temple with much fanfare to announce to the world he is the savior and god of this world.

I would encourage you to read all of Mark 13:14-27. I will write out the first and last verses of this sequence of verses Mark 13:14, 27: *When you see the abomination that causes desolation standing where it does not belong - let the reader understand - then let those who are in Judea flee to the mountains. . . . And he will send his angels and gather his elect from the four winds, from the ends of the earth to the ends of the heavens.*

If you will carefully read the above verses, Mark 13:14-27, you will see that the Rapture occurs after we see the abomination that causes desolation standing where it does not belong. The Bible says when you see the antichrist standing in the temple, this will be the time of the Rapture. If the temple had not been rebuilt and the antichrist had not arrived at the temple, then the Rapture could not occur until those events happened, according to God's own Word. If you will read Daniel 9:27, you will see the timing of this event. Daniel 9:27: *"He will confirm a covenant with many for one "seven," but in the middle of that "seven" he will put an end to sacrifice and offering. And one who causes desolation will place abomination on a wing of the temple until the end that is decreed is poured out on him.*

To me, this is plain speak. If the seven is the seven years of the Great Tribulation, and in the middle of the seven years is three and one-half years, then when you take Mark 13:14, 27 and Daniel 9:27 together, God's word plainly says that the Rapture will happen in the middle of the Great Tribulation.

After the Rapture, there is a great leadership vacuum in Israel because many Jews accepted Christ as their savior and went up in the Rapture. This has given the antichrist the opportunity he desired to make his move and set himself up as the god of this world. He does not quite get it. Jesus is coming back, and satan will lose.

2017 – 2020

The Rapture has happened. The bride of Christ has now been led to the throne of God, and a great celebration is happening. All those who would decide to make Christ their Lord have made that decision. Jesus waited until all who would accept Him made the right choice. Those people left behind are the ones who will later curse God as the wrath of God comes upon the earth and mankind.

Many Jews and Muslims accepted Christ as their Messiah before the Rapture as they are also an important part of Christ's bride. Those Jews who did not make that choice will have a hard time as the antichrist breaks his seven-year peace pact with Israel. The antichrist makes a shrewd decision not to make war on the Jews while simultaneously going after the saints. His peace pact with Israel makes it possible for him to focus his attention on the saints, and it gives the Jews a period of peace to rebuild the temple.

After the Rapture, the antichrist is left very frustrated, as the saints have been taken out of his reach. The 144,000 Jewish evangelists are working hard now to help warn and get the Jews around the world to a place of safety in Israel. Revelation 18:4 says, *Then I heard another voice from heaven say, "Come out of her my people, so that you will not share in her sins, so that you will not receive any of her plagues."* All hell is about to break loose as God pours out His wrath on the earth and unrepentant man. After a time of great celebration at the marriage supper of the Lamb, the bride of Christ will come back with Jesus Christ for the grand finale at the battle of Armageddon. Jude 14 : *Enoch the seventh from Adam, prophesied about these men: see the Lord is coming with thousands upon thousands of his holy ones.*

What totally amazes me is after the battle of Gog and Magog, where God showed the world what would happen to any nation who would try to attack God's chosen people the Jews, the nations of the world are about to try it again. This time, Jesus Himself, will lead the army that will put down all attempts to hurt Israel for the next 1000 years.

If you will read chapters 12-14 in Zechariah, you will see a complete picture of God's battle plan for the nations who would attack Israel, and you will see the ushering in of the millennial reign of Christ. What I will do is piece together some of the important verses from these three chapters, so you can see the unfolding of God's plan for both Israel and her enemies. What I am sharing here is not a scenario story; this is a commentary straight from God's Word.

I will start off with God's unshakable promise of protection for Israel. Zechariah 12:1-5: *This is the word of the Lord concerning Israel. The Lord, who stretches out the heavens, who lays the foundation of the earth, and who forms the spirit of man within him, declares: "I am going to make Jerusalem a cup that sends all the surrounding peoples reeling. Judah will be besieged as well as Jerusalem. On that day, when all the nations of the earth are gathered against her, I will make Jerusalem an immovable rock for all the nations. All who try to move it will injure themselves. On that day I will strike every horse with panic and its riders with madness,"* declares the Lord. *"I will keep a watchful eye over the house of Judah, but I will blind all the horses of the nations."* Then the leaders of Judah will say in their hearts, *"The people of Jerusalem are strong, because the Lord Almighty is their God. On that day men will be stricken by the Lord with great panic. Each man will seize the hand of another, and they will attack each other."*

These verses sound similar to what happens at the battle of Gog and Magog, but as you continue to read in your Bible, you will see the Lord is ushering in the 1000 years of peace. You will see that only a remnant totaling one-third of those Jews who were left behind in the Rapture will survive to live into the millennium. This one-third, who do survive these times, will totally turn back to the Lord in tears, realizing they were wrong.

Zechariah 12:10: *"And I will pour out on the house of David and the inhabitants of Jerusalem a spirit of grace and supplication. They will look on me, the one they have pierced, and they will mourn for him as one mourns for an only child, and grieve bitterly for him as one grieves for a first born son."*

In closing, the last two verses I use will be shortened for brevity, but if you will read these chapters yourself you will see I am staying true to the intended meaning. These verses show that the Lord is coming back to establish His kingdom on earth.

Zechariah 14:3-4b: *Then the Lord will go out and fight against those nations, as he fights in the day of battle. On that day his feet will stand on the Mount of Olives.*

Zechariah 14:5b: *Then the Lord my God will come, and all the holy ones with him.* **Praise the Lord, may you come quickly. We Win.**

— CHAPTER SIXTEEN —

HOW TO PREPARE
FOR THE LAST DAYS

If this study makes sense to you, you know we are fast approaching the coming of the Lord, and we will be going through part of the Great Tribulation. It begs the question, "What can we do to prepare for this time?" I will outline a few important steps we can take to prepare for what is coming soon.

1. Have you accepted Jesus Christ as your Savior?

If your answer is "yes," then the question is, "Are you living the Christian life to your full potential?" During these last days, God wants to use us to our fullest potential, and we must press in to seek God with all our hearts. Do some soul searching. This is where we have to really be honest with ourselves; we cannot hide anything from God. Do you have habits and sins that would be displeasing to God and hinder Him from using you?

As I bring this study to a close, I have felt the Holy Spirit leading me to include a study on the parable of the ten virgins. Jesus told this parable during His ministry on earth. It is found in Matthew 25:1-13; Jesus was teaching His disciples when they asked Him questions recorded in Matthew 24:3: *As Jesus was sitting on the Mount of Olives, the disciples came to him privately. "Tell us," they said, "when will this happen, and what will be the sign of your coming and the end of the age?"* Jesus went on to teach His disciples about His coming in Matthew 24 (much of it is in what I call plain-speak). When Jesus taught His disciples as recorded in chapter twenty-five, He spoke in parables. Jesus' disciples asked Him questions written in Matthew 13:10-11: *"Why do you speak to the people in parables?"* This was his reply, *"The knowledge of the secrets of the kingdom of heaven has been given to you, but not to them."* Jesus went on to say, *"There are those who have become calloused, and the truths of God's word are hidden from them."*

I have given this brief explanation on what a parable is because many parables are difficult to understand and not always explained in the Bible. I believe the parable of the ten virgins holds many insights concerning what will be happening at the time of Christ's return for His bride. I will write out the whole parable and give a brief running commentary on some of the message I believe God wants us to understand as we approach the time of Christ's return for His bride.

Matthew 25:1-13 says, *At that time the kingdom of heaven will be like ten virgins who took their lamps and went out to meet the bridegroom. Five of them were foolish and five were wise. The foolish ones took their lamps but did not take any oil with them. The wise, however, took oil in jars along with their lamps. The bridegroom was a long time in coming, and they all became drowsy and fell asleep. At midnight the cry rang out: "Here's the bridegroom! Come out to meet him!" Then all the virgins woke up and trimmed their lamps. The foolish ones said to the wise, "Give us some of your oil; our lamps are going out." "No," they replied, "there may not be enough for both us and you. Instead, go to those who sell oil and buy some for yourselves." But while they were on their way to buy oil, the bridegroom arrived. The virgins who were ready went in with him to the wedding banquet. And the door was shut. Later the others also came. "Sir! Sir!" they said. "Open the door for us!" But he replied, "I tell you the truth, I don't know you." Therefore keep watch, because you do not know the day or the hour.*

To start off, I did a study on the significance of the number ten.

According to Jewish custom, if you have ten Jews living together, you have a congregation, and you can build a synagogue. This truth indicates to me that Jesus was talking about the church as well as a Jewish synagogue. With this in mind, you realize Jesus was saying at the time of the end, when the church is waiting for His coming, many in the church will have similar traits to the ten virgins. There is much significance to the fact they were carrying lamps that needed oil to be ready for the bridegroom's return. The lamps were the vessels that held the oil. When you study the Bible, you learn the oil is symbolic of the Holy Spirit, and we are the vessels in which the Holy Spirit lives.

This parable says the five foolish virgins did not even have any oil. As Christians, the oil of the Holy Spirit is what gives us our power and strength to live the Christian life. I believe that those believers who do not have any oil are not taking their walk with God seriously. They may be going to church, but they are really just going through the motions.

When the Bible says the bridegroom was a long time in coming, I believe it is saying Christ's return has not happened as soon as many expected. I believe, after having done this whole study on the end times, that eighty to ninety percent of American Christians, who have been taught Christ is coming before the antichrist arrives followed by the seven-year tribulation, will be in for a big surprise. I believe the strongest message from this parable is for those who are not taking their walk with God seriously and will be too weak to make it to the end.

Job in the Old Testament story went through the greatest tribulation any man has ever had to suffer. His wife even told him to just curse God and die. Many a man in his day would not have stayed true to God, but Job's walk and faith in God were stronger than any storm or trial that came his way. I believe many Christians going through the coming tribulations of the last days will only make it because they will have an inner strength from the Spirit of God, similar to what Job had. This strength of the Spirit can only be developed by spending time with God in His Word and in prayer. Just showing up at church once a week will not develop the strength of spirit we will need to weather the storms ahead. My last closing thought may raise some eyebrows, but I will speak my mind, for I believe what I am about to say needs to be said. At the end of the parable when the five foolish virgins went on their way to find the oil they needed and later came back wanting to enter the marriage supper, Jesus said, *"I tell you the truth, I don't know you."* **As I was studying this, I wondered what could the five foolish virgins have done that was so bad that they would be totally rejected. What this parable is saying is many people in the church will not make it into the kingdom of God. In fact, it shows that fifty percent will not make it. <u>This is serious</u>. What can this possibly mean?**

As I have studied and prayed over this, I have come up with only one answer. The Bible talks about a sin that is unpardonable. It is referred to as blasphemy against the Holy Spirit. I have heard teaching that considers taking one's own life is also unpardonable. Well, I believe in the last days there is another unpardonable sin, and that is to take the mark of the beast. I believe, in the last days, when we are going through the tribulation before the wrath of God begins, this portion of the last days will be a time of testing for Christians unlike anything we have ever seen here in America. I believe the weight of scripture shows the church will have to make the choice of whether or not to accept the antichrist's system. We will be amply warned not to take the mark of the beast, but I believe many churches are full of weak Christians, and many of these will say, "God would not expect them to go hungry and die." I believe they could be easily deceived into believing the antichrist is their savior and go along with his system. The bottom line is, unless we are full of the Spirit of God and have the strength of the Spirit that will carry us through these times of trials and tribulations that lie ahead, we could end up being like the foolish virgins who do not make it into the marriage supper of the Lamb. I am listing a few Scripture references below that go along with what I am saying in this study on the ten virgins. I encourage you to look them up and see if what I am saying is plausible.

God warns the saints not to take the mark of the beast... Revelation 14:9-12

Why the Lord delays His coming... 2 Peter 3:9

God warns saints to be patient... Revelation 13:9-10

War on saints to last three and one-half years... Daniel 7:25

If you have not accepted Jesus as your Lord and Savior, these easy steps will put you in right standing with God.

1. Admit you are a sinner and repent.

Romans 3:10: *As it is written: there is no one righteous, not even one.*

Romans 3:23: *For all have sinned and fall short of the glory of God.*

Luke 5:32: *I have not come to call the righteous, but sinners to repentance.*

2. Believe in the Lord Jesus Christ.

John 3:16: *For God so loved the world that he gave his one and only Son, that whosoever believes in him shall not perish but have eternal life.*

3. Confess or declare that Jesus is the Lord of your life.

Romans 10:9: *That if you confess with your mouth, "Jesus is Lord," and believe in your heart that God raised him from the dead, you shall be saved.*

THE SINNER'S PRAYER

If you would like God to forgive all your sins and make Jesus Christ the

Lord of your life, then stop here and say this prayer to God. (Prayer is simply talking to God.)

Dear Heavenly Father, I know I am a sinner. I believe Jesus Christ died on the cross for me. Please forgive me of all my sins. Jesus, please come into my heart and wash my sins away. Please be the Lord of my life and help me to live for you every day. I ask this in Jesus' name. Amen.

The Bible says when a sinner repents and makes Jesus his Lord, the angels in heaven rejoice.

A word of warning is advised at this point. As we read in the story of the ten virgins, not all who call themselves Christians will make it to heaven. Knowing about Jesus and the plan of salvation is no guarantee of making it to heaven. When we arrive in heaven, the greatest surprise will be seeing people we did not think would make it. And just as surprising will be the absence of those we thought would be there. The Bible says Jesus knocks on the door of our hearts and wants to come in and live with us. The important thing to realize is God wants our hearts, not just our minds. Head knowledge about salvation does not save us, but sincerely allowing God to forgive and wash our sins away will allow God to give you a new heart. When your heart is changed, people will notice you have been changed and made into a new person in Christ. This is called being "Born Again."

I would like to share a story from a recent conversation I had with a young man who believes we really are close to the Lord's return. He told me he would never take the mark of the beast. Yet he believes it's acceptable for him to live with his girlfriend and go out and get drunk from time to time. He has what I call "designer faith." It is NOT based on the pure Word of God, but it is based on what seems good to him. What a shame it would be for someone to go through the Tribulation of the last days and refuse to take the mark of the beast and then still not make it into the Kingdom of Heaven because they did not have a true born again experience, based on the Word of God.

As a new believer, your next step would be for you to find a network of believers to help you grow in the Lord. Finding a good church is a good place to start.

2. Is your financial house in order?

This question requires taking steps to streamline your budget and get out of debt, if at all possible. Even Christians have been wasting money and living beyond their means. Based on my study of God's Word, I believe the beginning of the Great Tribulation could be only three to seven years away. When I started this study two years ago, I realized I had assets I could use to help me get out of debt. I went through my credit card bills and looked for recurring monthly bills I could cut from my budget. I personally eliminated three hundred dollars a month through this process. A lot more can be said in this category, but the bottom line is, as we approach the Lord's coming, we will witness the world and society being turned upside down as we know it. The opportunities to witness to the backsliders and the lost will be tremendous. Those who get their financial house in order will be in the best position to reach out to the lost during these times.

Under the subject of finances, I cannot believe how many financial advisors are telling people to put their resources into gold and silver. I do not believe we will ever see gold and silver become the medium of exchange in America or the world. How do you split a gold coin to buy food? If you think about it, the thing that really drives up the value of precious metals is fear. The fear that the value of our currency will collapse and become worthless. This did not even happen during the Great Depression. Now I am not saying this could not happen. In fact, I believe we are heading towards a global economic collapse, and this event will lead to the formation of a one-world government. I believe this event must happen before the antichrist can rise to power. So, as a Christian, I want to know what God's Word has to say about my investments. Ezekiel 7:19 says, *They shall cast their silver in the streets and their gold shall not be able to deliver them in the day of the wrath of Lord. They shall not satisfy their souls, neither fill their bowels.* Then read Zephaniah 1:18: *Neither their silver, nor their gold, will be able to save them on the day of the Lord's wrath.*

Think about this, as we approach the Lord's coming and the global famines that will take place as described in the opening of the seals of Revelation 6, people who have prepared and have food will not want your gold for their food. As Ezekiel 7:19 says, *..they shall not satisfy their souls, neither fill their bowels...* Bowels are your belly. To me, God's Word is saying it is wiser to have food for your belly than to have gold. You could even say during these coming hard times that food will be gold.

The other day I was reading headlines on the internet. One headline from a financial advisor, Paul Mladjenovic, had a title that caught my attention. When I opened the link, it said he wanted everyone to consider three simple things to gain greater financial peace of mind:

1. Diversify away from paper assets.

2. Accumulate essentials

3. Refocus your portfolio with emphasis on "Human Need."

His second item, coming from a non-Christian perspective, really caught my attention. He said, "Accumulate essentials." He went on to say, "As odd as this may sound for some of you, consider starting a pantry or otherwise consider stocking up on essentials such as non-perishable foods, extra water, etc. NO, I am not asking you to become a survivalist or a hermit. I consider this to be just another form of diversification. The world is too precarious right now and is quite vulnerable to disruptions. Severe inflation is not far off. Potential problems can come from a variety of expected and unexpected venues. What do you think will have greater value a few years from now, a dollar or a can of soup?" I think this is sound advice for anyone. I could not have said it better.

3. What pastors can do to prepare their church.

As pastors, you have an important responsibility to teach your flock to be ready for the last days. I am not just talking about having food pantries stocked, but you must provide leadership and hope to your people. If you fall short in this area or you wait until it's too late to prepare, your people will blame you. When the Titanic was sinking, many people were in a state of panic because the ship was not prepared for its last day.

As the pastor of a church, you should consider starting home cell Bible studies or cell groups. I believe as persecution grows against the church and Christians, we will need to go underground. Already under our newly elected president, there is talk of eliminating churches' tax-exempt status and eliminating tax deductions for giving to churches and charities. If our country and the world go into a time of global economic collapse as we approach the Lord's coming, it is easy to see the high tax burden being assessed on churches will cause many to go bankrupt, forcing churches to move into homes. Also, home cells can be very effective in bringing the lost to a saving knowledge of Christ. When things start falling apart in our society and our economy collapses, and when the government is not there to meet every need the people have, it will be the close friendships that will develop in the small group settings that will make your Christian friends closer than a brother who will be there when you are in need.

I believe pastors hold a unique responsibility to help prepare their flock for what is to come. Pastors should realize the church will be in for horrendous hard times before the Lord returns. I believe churches should lead by example and have a food pantry for the needy. They should encourage their people to use a portion of their resources to lay aside essentials for the hard times ahead. Proverbs 21:20 states, *In the house of the wise are stores of choice food and oil, but the foolish man devours all he has.*

If what I say in this book makes sense, but you take no action to

warn and prepare your church, it's no different than not having read this message at all. Once the truth of this book becomes evident to all, it will be too late to get ready.

I believe in the years ahead leading up to the return of Christ for His bride, the church, or better yet the saints in the churches, will be responsible to preach the gospel to their lost or backslidden family, friends, and neighbors. We should have extra Bibles. I believe God's Word says there will be a famine of the Word of God in the last days, and we should be prepared while there are no limits on how many Bibles, hymnals, and songbooks we can have.

4. Food storage and gardening.

So much can be said under this subject. The Bible clearly predicts food will be scarce in the last days, and many will die of famine and starvation. I believe many Christians, who have been told the Rapture will come before the Great Tribulation starts, will turn bitter towards God and the church. I believe they will be part of a great falling away. The Bible also says there will be a great revival in the last days as well.

Esau gave up his birthright for a bowl of soup, and I am afraid many Christians who fall away in the last days will be the ones unprepared for a time of Great Tribulation. When they are offered an opportunity to buy into the system of the antichrist for food, they will succumb. Many Christians in America do not believe we will see famine on our shores. If this is what you think, you will be in for a big surprise. We are more dependent on our food coming from foreign lands now than anytime in American history. Not only does our food come from places like Canada, Mexico, and South America, but many of the local farms that produce the food for the local market have been turned into housing developments or Wal-Marts.

I believe we need to learn how to grow food in our own gardens. Stored food will run out, but if you learn to grow your own food, you will have food for your daily needs. Most people have not learned how to raise their own food. We are too dependent on stocked shelves in our grocery stores. If you do not know how to garden, do not wait to learn. Start practicing now. **Do not wait until it is too late to buy garden tools, seeds, and other garden supplies. Remember: learning how to can your crops and having sufficient canning supplies on hand is an important part of having a garden.**

We should look at the Mormons. They have been taught to prepare for hard times. They are told they should have at least a year's worth of food stored for unexpected calamities, whether it is losing a job or widespread hard times.

Today, with all the natural disasters and economic turmoil in this country and around the world, the Red Cross is recommending that we have seven days of food and water on hand in case of an emergency. If what you are reading in this study makes sense to you, then I hope you realize that seven days of food and water will not cut it. How much preparation is necessary? This is something we need to seek God about while we pray for His wisdom and guidance.

Some Christians say the Bible says to "take no thought for tomorrow." Stop and think about this. There have been extraordinary times in history when these words did not apply. Before the flood, God prompted Noah to prepare. Read Hebrews 11:7: ***By faith Noah, when warned about things not yet seen, in holy fear built an ark to save his family.*** God showed Joseph that Egypt was to prepare during good times for a seven-year famine to come. There was a time in the New Testament when the Christians had things in common during hard times, but how can Christians share if they do not have anything to share?

Wouldn't you agree that the coming of the Lord, with the catastrophic events leading up to His return, will be extraordinary times? Today, we are witnessing economic earthquakes that are shaking and taking down countries around the world. Millions are losing their homes to foreclosure. Many are losing all they have worked years to accumulate.

I know Christians who are up to their ears in debt, trying to hold onto multiple assets and homes that are more than they can afford. Many are holding on tightly, hoping some bailout will rescue them. I am praying we will see an economic turn-around, and if this happens, I pray the church will realize we have been seeing the birth pains leading up to the coming of the Lord and recognize time is short. We need to take the short time we have to consolidate our debts and pay off our homes, if possible. Turn off the television and turn God's Word on in our lives. Let God show you what you need to do with the short time we have before His coming.

I want to encourage the readers of this book to consider obtaining a food and preparedness insurance policy. If you buy a home, there may be less than one in a thousand odds your home will burn down, but you are required by the bank to have a fire insurance policy. If you buy a car and drive, even though the chances of having an accident are less than one in a thousand, you are required to have an auto insurance policy. Now, if you have studied along with me and agree, we are seeing unprecedented times and cataclysmic events that are sending clouds of uncertainty around the world. You must realize before the world or America will be willing to agree to join a one-world government, America will have to experience economic and social collapse. The will of the world to resist change will be broken. If you believe as I do that the odds of these things happening before the Lord's return are at least fifty-fifty, why not acquire a preparedness insurance policy? I hope your response will not be what I heard from one pastor, "Why store food or have a garden? Others will only steal it from you anyway." It is a good thing Noah or Joseph did not have that attitude.

In closing, I would like to encourage you to start buying extra food items on a weekly basis. I find that, if I shop the sales, when I see certain canned goods at a good price, I will buy ten instead of two. With frugal buying, you will discover you can accumulate quite a pantry without expanding your food budget. I recently figured out that for $300 you can buy enough food for one person for a year at a box store such as

Costco. I'm talking about food that will store well for years, like rice, beans, oatmeal, and other items to compliment a simple diet that will keep you alive on a low budget. If you have the financial resources, you should consider buying food that is packaged to last from ten to twenty years or more. Again there are creative ways to find the money you need to make this type of investment. Maybe it is time to sell the boat, the motorcycle or some other cherished item that you will not need when your way of life has been turned upside down. Below I will list four sources for long term food. Realize that your grocery store is a good source as well as the discount box stores. I have read studies that have shown that regular canned goods stored in a cool place are still good to eat after thirty years with very little taste and nutrient loss.

Jim Bakker Ministries. They sell food packages that come in large buckets that are freeze dried products that will last for twenty years. I believe some of their packages are the best value per serving that can be found. You can contact them at 417-779-9000. Their internet address is www.jimbakkershow.com/shop

Nitro-Pak. This company sells a vast assortment of food and preparedness products. They are distributors for the Mountain House brand of freeze dried food; this is truly the gourmet of long term food. This product is the same product you buy in camping stores. You only need to add boiling water, and in ten minutes, your meal is ready to eat. You may reach them at 800-866-4876 or on the internet at www. nitro-pak.com.

Ready Made Resources. This company is probably the biggest resource for both long term food and preparedness products that you could find. They sell packages that will be balanced with dehydrated, freeze dried and whole grains for long term storage. I have talked to the owner of this company, and he is very much committed to helping Christians prepare for hard times ahead. You can reach this company at 800-627-3809 or on the internet at www.readymaderesources.com.

911 Food and Water. This company is an emergency preparedness provider born out of years of study on Biblical prophecy. It is operated on the Joseph Principal. As you buy your food and preparedness products to protect your family, they send a percentage of free food to your church, to help your church stock their food pantry to help those who were not able to prepare. You can reach this company at 855-511-0911 or online at www.911foodandwater.com.

— CHAPTER SEVENTEEN —

CLOSING THOUGHTS ABOUT THE LORD'S RETURN

The Bible says the weapons of our warfare are powerful through God for the pulling down of strongholds. In the last days, and I am talking about now, God is raising up an army. This army must not shrink back from the task ahead. God's army will be fully equipped with God's most powerful weapons, but if we shrink back, God is not pleased. If we do not appropriate the weapons God has made available, we will not be prepared for what lies ahead.

I remember as a teenager visiting the Winchester Gun Museum in New Haven, Connecticut. I was so intrigued to see the Gatlin gun. I still have a picture I took of this awesome weapon. The weapon display gave some background information I have never forgotten. It said this model of Gatlin gun was made available to General Custer. This gun could shoot two hundred rounds a minute, and when General Custer received word he should take it with him to Little Big Horn, his response was "It would just slow me down." So he went charging out to meet the enemy, and when he found himself surrounded, he must have thought, "I have two hundred Indians a minute more than I can handle. Why didn't I bring that gun?" Well, it was too late for him at that point.

The Bible says the weapons of our warfare are powerful for the pulling down of strongholds. There is a weapon in the arsenal of God like the Gatlin gun, and it is often left behind. This weapon is prayer and fasting. I would like to share a couple of stories of how I learned about how prayer and fasting can greatly benefit your life.

Back in the early seventies when I was saved, I was working in a logging camp for most of the year, then I would attend college in the winters. Before I attended Bible college, I was going to college at the University of Alaska in Fairbanks. While going to school, I attended Fairbanks First Assembly of God. I received some good teaching on prayer and fasting, and I started taking time to fast and pray while I was attending school. At that time, I did not have many struggles, but I sensed God was doing good things in my life. I transferred to Northwest Bible College. After a few years in attendance there, I became concerned because I had not met the woman of my life. So before going back to college for my third year, I started fasting and praying seriously for God to bring that special person into my life. When I went back to Northwest College in 1977, I met Shawnette Rasmussen, who would later become my wife.

When I look back, I can see God's hand powerfully involved in bringing us together. Shawnette was six years younger than me. I did not really want to pursue a girl this young, but God kept bringing her across my path. Before long, I had to ask God if He was trying to tell me something. I remember thinking that I needed to keep an open mind as I did not want to miss God's will. God gave me many confirmations that it was okay to pursue this neat, cute girl. Before long, I had an opportunity to meet her grandparents, who drove down from Canada to visit her. They invited us to drive up for Thanksgiving, and God gave me special favor with them. When her parents got together with her grandparents for Christmas, Shawnette's grandparents could not quit talking about me. I met her parents when they dropped Shawnette off at college after Christmas break. Again, God gave me favor with her dad.

Our marriage has been good, and I would not trade Shawnette for any girl in the world. I am totally convinced that Shawnette came into my life because I fasted and prayed. When I did my part to let God know that I wanted His best for my life, then He made all the arrangements to bring the most perfect girl my way.

You would think that I would have learned a great lesson here, but the truth is I hardly fasted after seeing God answering my requests from prayer and fasting. I believe I was just too comfortable. During the last two to three years, I have rediscovered the power of prayer and fasting. As we have been seeing our country enter a period of economic hardship, I have been up against a wall financially several times. But for the last three years, as I have fasted and prayed for my needs and have sought God for His will in my life, God has come through every time. During this process of rediscovering the power of prayer and fasting, it is almost like I have rediscovered how great and loving our God is and how much He wants to have a close relationship with us individually. In these last days, we will have trying times. We need to seek God like we never have before. As we press into God, we will discover how great and loving our heavenly Father really is and how much He wants to protect us and meet our every need. We must never lose sight of God's love for us. John 3:16: *For God so loved the world that he gave his one and only Son, that whosoever believes in him shall not perish but have eternal life.*

Imagine this: God is giving His church a last chance to finish the Great Commission and preach the gospel to the millions who will be seeing hard times. As we are approaching the Great Tribulation, there will be many lost and confused souls who will want to know where to turn. Remember when 911 hit, and the churches were full for a week or two? When the Great Tribulation gets started, and the seals start to pop open, the global events that will be taking place will make 911 and the Twin Towers look like a picnic. When 911 hit, our churches filled up for two weeks and then emptied again. When the coming economic collapse happens, it will be like 911 again, but it won't go away in two weeks.

Try to imagine the church being raptured before any of this happens. On the following Sunday, the churches fill up to overflowing, just as they did after 911. All these millions will fill up our churches to get answers, and they will be open to hear the gospel. What will they find? All the pastors have been raptured and only the returning backsliders and lukewarm Christians are left to lead these millions to the Lord (the lukewarm Christians who skipped out of Sunday School and have not studied their Bibles and do not have the answers.) So, we have two scenarios here. We can hold to a pre-tribulation rapture view and believe the saints, involved in the "war on the saints" described in the book of Revelation, will be the ones the Bible depicts as the triumphant church. This church will be made up of all the lukewarm Christians and repentant backsliders who were left behind but now are on fire for God. Those people would end up becoming the church, tried by fire, for which Christ is coming back. Or the second option: the Rapture is a mid-tribulation rapture, and we are prepared to help our unprepared family, friends, and neighbors by ministering to the needs of the lost and hungry, so that many will be saved, for we are still here and not yet raptured.

As I have said, I would rather see a pre-tribulation rapture. It would be so much easier for me and all of us Christians. Wait a minute; does God's Word not say God is unwilling that any should perish? If the Rapture is a pre-tribulation event, and it were to happen tonight while you were sleeping, what would it be like to stand before Christ, the one who gave His life that all could be saved? You have just entered the glorious gates of heaven; you have no doubt your eternity is secure. What would you do if Jesus were to ask you, "Did you do all you could to tell others about me before you left?" If Jesus could give you a choice to stay in heaven or go back and have a part in the greatest evangelistic opportunity in history, what would your choice be?

I was recently watching a movie called *Schindler's List* about a German business man named Oscar Schindler who organized and ran his factories with cheap Jewish labor. When he started, his motives were purely based on greed. As the war went on, he developed a love for the Jewish people, and he used all his wealth and influence to bribe the Nazi officials and save his workers from the death camps. When the day came that the war was over and the Jewish people were set free, those whose lives he saved wanted to give him a gift. They pulled out their teeth which had gold fillings and made a ring for Oscar Schindler. He cried, "I could have saved more." When we get to heaven, it will be the same. Those whose lives you had a part in getting to heaven will be your best friends for eternity. We will also cry, knowing we could have helped more people get to heaven.

I believe the church must wake up to the facts that they will not have a future secured by their retirement plans, their only hope is in Christ, and they are in the final countdown. This awakening will lead to the greatest revival the world has ever seen. As the revelation of Christ's coming sinks in, it will finally hit home that only what is done for Christ will last.

I am afraid that the church of today is not ready for what is before us. When prophetic events soon begin to unfold and the timing of the Rapture does not happen as we have been taught, this error will lead to great confusion. Many believers will rise to the occasion as Jesus' disciples did when given a choice by Christ to leave Him. They said, "ONLY YOU HAVE THE WORDS OF ETERNAL LIFE." On the other hand, many in the church will feel God has abandoned them to suffer on the earth during this time, and their bitterness will cause many to turn away from Christ.

I was recently visiting a pastor and talking to him about my book. Before we parted, he told a story he had heard from a pastor friend who shared my view of a mid-tribulation rapture. This pastor shared this story about a tribe in Northern Africa that had two churches, each teaching a different position concerning the coming of the Lord.

One of the missionaries to this tribe taught that the Lord was coming soon, and they did not have to worry about going through a time of great tribulation. They would all be raptured out before things became very bad. The second missionary taught those in his church that we would see a period of Great Tribulation before the Lord returns. Some may even die, but God's grace would carry them through any trials or tribulations they would face.

This area came under attack by terrorists. Many died from both churches. The church that was taught not to worry about trials and tribulation was devastated. Many left the church and lost their faith in God. The church that was taught that they would have to face trials and tribulations came out stronger in their faith than they were before. I am afraid for the church in America which has been taught that before things get bad, we are "out of here." Please pray with me that the message of this book will travel rapidly and that its readers would have an open heart to receive its message.

If I am correct in this study that the church is to go through the first half of the Great Tribulation, we need to realize God does not want His church to suffer through part of the Great Tribulation for no reason. No! God wants His church to be a <u>victorious</u> church and to show Satan His church will not retreat with its tail tucked in. No! We will rise to the occasion and do exploits for God, and in the end, it will be Satan who will lose. I believe we will be the victorious church God will use to reach out and snatch the lost out of Satan's grasp. Every time we lead a lost soul to Christ, it is like we have punched Satan in the nose. The salvation of those lost souls will make it worth any suffering we have to endure. Sure, we will have casualties, but we will win the war!

I was watching the movie *Titanic* the other day, and this spiritual thought about the last days came to me. I watched the minister on board moving among those who were not able to get on a lifeboat; these were people who knew they were facing certain death. The minister was not looking for a way onto a lifeboat because he knew he had a lifeboat in Christ Jesus. At the end of the movie, reportedly, most of the lifeboats were only half full, and the fortunate ones who were in lifeboats could have gone back and helped those who were in the water drowning. This inaction led to a lifetime of guilt.

In closing, as we approach the last of the last days, do we want to head for home with our lifeboat half full? Our reward is secure, so why should we be in such a hurry to head for home?

May we be ready for His Coming!

John Shorey

reorder information on the following page

If you believe in the message of this book and would like to share in the ministry of getting this important message out, please consider taking a part by:

- Writing about *The Window of the Lord's Return* on your blog, Twitter, MySpace, and Facebook page.

- Suggesting *The Window of the Lord's Return* to friends and send then to the books website **www.tribulationtruth.com**.

- When you're in a bookstore, ask them if they carry the book. The book is available through all major distributors, so any bookstore that does not have it in stock can easily order it.

- Writing a positive review on www.amazon.com.

- Purchasing additional copies to give away as gifts.

You can order additional copies of the book from my website by going to **www.tribulationtruth.com**. Special bulk quantity discounts are available.

Other teaching aids available at: **www.tribulationtruth.com**.

Recently, I did a series of television tapings where I clearly and visually outlined the highlights from my book. This is vital information I believe you and your family will want to see and share with family and friends. To order this DVD, go to my website: **www.tribulationtruth. com**

SPEAKING SCHEDULE

I am available to share the insights God has directed me to write in this Book. To contact me concerning speaking and preaching engagements, I may be reached through my web site: **www.tribulationtruth.com**.